AQA

Biology AS
Student Workbook

Model Answers: 2011

This model answer book is a companion publication to provide answers for the exercises in the **AQA AS Biology Student Workbook** 2011 edition. These answers have been produced as a separate publication to keep the cost of the workbook itself to a minimum, as well as to prevent easy access to the answers by students. In most cases, simply the answer is given with no working or calculations described. A few, however, have been provided with more detail because of their difficult nature.

ISBN 978-1-877462-67-2

Copyright © 2010 Richard Allan
Published by BIOZONE International Ltd

www.biozone.co.uk

BIOZONE

Additional copies of this Model Answers book may be purchased directly from the publisher

UK & EUROPE:
BIOZONE Learning Media (UK) Ltd.
Bretby Business Park, Ashby Road, Bretby,
Burton upon Trent, DE15 0YZ, **UK**
Telephone: 01283-553-257
Fax: 01283-553-258
Email: sales@biozone.co.uk

AUSTRALIA:
BIOZONE Learning Media Australia
P.O. Box 2841, Burleigh BC,
QLD 4220, **Australia**
Telephone: +61 7-5535-4896
Fax: +61 7-5508-2432
Email: sales@biozone.com.au

REST OF WORLD:
BIOZONE International Ltd.
P.O. Box 13-034,
Hamilton 3251, **New Zealand**
Telephone: +64 7-856-8104
Fax: +64 7-856-9243
Email: sales@biozone.co.nz

Contents

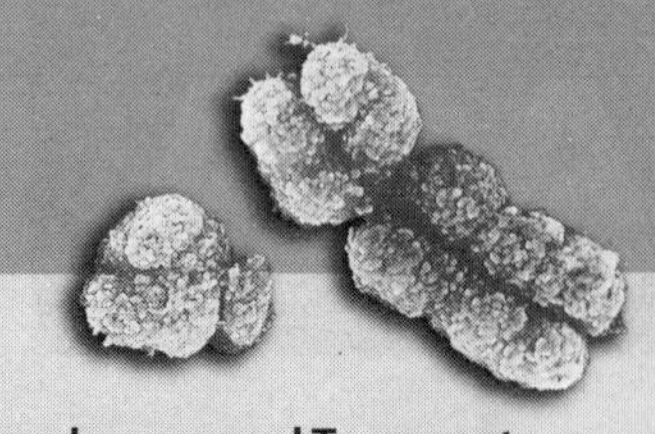

Contents

Contents

Classification and Evidence of Phylogeny

Evolution and Biodiversity

Hypotheses and Predictions (page 9)

1. Prediction: Woodlice are more likely to be found in moist habitats than in dry habitats.

2. (a) **Bacterial cultures**:
   Prediction: Bacterial strain A will grow more rapidly at 37°C than at room temperature (19°C).
   Outline of the investigation: Set up agar plates of bacterial strain A, using the streak plating method. Place 4 plates in a 37°C incubator and 4 on the lab bench. Leave all 8 plates for the same length of time (e.g. 24 hours), with all other conditions identical. Measure the coverage of the agar plates with bacteria (as a percentage).
   (b) **Plant cloning**:
   Prediction: A greater concentration of hormone A increases the rate of root growth in plant A.
   Outline of the investigation: Set up 6 agar plates infused with increasing concentrations of hormone A (e.g. 1 mgl^{-1}, 5 mgl^{-1}, 10 mgl^{-1}, 50 mgl^{-1}, 100 mgl^{-1}, 500 mgl^{-1}), and each plate with 12 clones of plant A. Measure root length each day for 20 days.

A Qualititative Practical Task (page 12)

1. (a) All samples had to be heated for the same amount of time to ensure they all received the same treatment conditions for reaction.
   (b) Stirring ensures maximum contact of substrate and enzyme therefore maximising reaction.

2. As the bananas ripen, the starch is converted to simple sugars fructose and glucose.

3. (a) Fructose is a ketose sugar, but it is converted to glucose in the basic reagent and the aldehyde group gives a positive test.
   (b) You cannot tell from the test results if the banana ripening resulted in conversion of starch to glucose alone or to fructose (fruit sugar) and glucose (in fact it is converted to both).

A Quantitative Practical Task (page 13)

1. Aim: To investigate the effect of temperature on the rate of catalase activity.

2. Hypothesis: The rate of catalase activity is dependent on temperature.

3. (a) Independent variable: Temperature.
   (b) Values: 10-60°C in uneven steps: 10°C, 20°C, 30°C, 60°C.
   (c) Unit: °C
   (d) Equipment: A means to maintain the test-tubes at the set temperatures, e.g. water baths. Equilibrate all reactants to the required temperatures in each case, before adding enzyme to the reaction tubes.

4. (a) Dependent variable: Height of oxygen bubbles.
   (b) Unit: mm
   (c) Equipment: Ruler; place vertically alongside the tube and read off the height (directly facing).

5. (a) Each temperature represents a treatment.
   (b) No. of tubes at each temperature = 2
   (c) Sample size: for each treatment = 2
   (d) Times the investigation repeated = 3

6. It would have been desirable to have had an extra tube with no enzyme to determine whether or not any oxygen was produced in the absence of enzyme.

7. Variables that might have been controlled (a-c):
   (a) Catalase from the same batch source and with the same storage history. Likewise for the H_2O_2. Storage and batch history can be determined.
   (b) Equipment of the same type and size (i.e. using test-tubes of the same dimensions, as well as volume). This could be checked before starting.
   (c) Same person doing the measurements of height each time. This should be decided beforehand.

   Note that some variables were controlled: The test-tube volume, and the volume of each reactant. Control of measurement error is probably the most important after these considerations.

8. Controlled variables should be monitored carefully to ensure that the only variable that changes between treatments (apart from the biological response) is the independent (manipulated) variable.

Recording Results (page 15)

1. See the results table at the top of the next page.

2. The table would be three times as big in the vertical dimension; the layout of the top of the table would be unchanged. The increased vertical height of the table would accommodate the different ranges of the independent variable (full light, as in question 1, but also half light, and low light. These ranges would have measured (quantified) values attached to them.

Variables and Data (page 16)

1. Measure wavelength (in nm) using a spectrophotometer; which measures light intensity as a function of the colour (wavelength) of light.

2. These data are semi-quantitative because an arbitrary numerical value has been assigned to a qualitative scale. The numbers are correct in a relative sense, but do not necessarily indicate the true quantitative values.

Manipulating Raw Data (page 17)

1. Basic transformations of raw data identify important features (e.g. trends) of the data.
   Data transformation can identify trends early on. Often these transformations can help a researcher to set the direction for subsequent experimental work.

2. (a) Percentage.
   (b) Allows you to compare the relative number of species at each habitat.

3.

Incidence of cyanogenic clover in different areas

Clover plant type	Frost free area		Frost prone area		
	Number	%	Number	%	Totals
Cyanogenic	120	76	22	15	142
Acyanogenic	38	24	120	85	158
Total	158	100	142	100	300

		Trial 1 / CO$_2$ conc. in ppm											Trial 2 / CO$_2$ conc. in ppm											Trial 3 / CO$_2$ conc. in ppm										
						Minutes											Minutes											Minutes						
	Set up no.	0	1	2	3	4	5	6	7	8	9	10	0	1	2	3	4	5	6	7	8	9	10	0	1	2	3	4	5	6	7	8	9	10
Full light conditions	1																																		
	2																																		
	3																																		
	Av.																																		

Constructing Tables (page 18)

1. (a)-(b) any two of the following (all for achieved):
   - Tables provide a systematic record of information.
   - Tables provide a way of condensing data.
   - Tables provide a summary of results.
   - Tables show trends and relationships in the data.

2. To identify trends in the data. To help decide the best method of graphing the data.

3. (a) Allows the data to be summarised so that trends or patterns can be identified more easily than by presenting raw data alone. It also aids the researcher in deciding the best way to graph the data to show the trend.
   (b) Allows the researcher to determine if the data is normally distributed or skewed. This will determine how the data will be further manipulated.

4. So that the control values are easily identified and compared with the values obtained for the treatments. This allows the researcher and readers to determine if the treatments are having any real effect.

Constructing Graphs (page 19)

1. Graphs visually show a trend or relationship in data using a minimum of space.

2. (a) Appropriate scale shows the trend in the data most clearly. For example, if the scale is too compressed then it is difficult to see the trend.
   (b) A floating or broken axis may be used when there is a large gap between zero and where the data begins. This allows for the data trends to be more easily visualised.

3. (a) The time intervals on the X-axis are evenly spaced even though the time increments at which the data were recorded are not.
   (b) If the graph were plotted correctly then the data points would be stretched out. When the line of best fit was applied the slope of the plotted data would be much flatter than the original.

Drawing Bar Graphs (page 20)

1. (a) Table as below:

Species	Site 1	Site 2
Ornate limpet	21	30
Radiate limpet	6	34
Limpet sp. A	38	-
Limpet sp. B	57	39
Limpet sp. C	-	2
Catseye	6	2
Topshell	2	4
Chiton	1	3

   (b) Bar graph: *See the next page of graph solutions.*

Drawing Histograms (page 21)

1. (a) Tally chart totals as below:

Weight group	Total
45-49.9	1
50-54.9	2
55-59.9	7 (given)
60-64.9	13
65-69.9	15
70-74.9	13
75-79.9	11
80-84.9	16
85-89.9	9
90-94.9	5
95-99.9	2
100-104.9	0
105-109.9	1

   (b) Histogram: *See the next page of graph solutions.*

Drawing Pie Graphs (page 22)

1. (a) Tabulated data:

Food item in diet	Stoats % in diet	Stoats Angle /°	Rats % in diet	Rats Angle /°	Cats % in diet	Cats Angle /°
Birds	23.6	85	1.4	5	6.9	25
Crickets	15.3	55	23.6	85	-	-
Insects	15.3	55	20.8	75	1.9	7
Voles	9.2	33	-	-	19.4	70
Rabbits	8.3	30	-	-	18.1	65
Rats	6.1	22	-	-	43.1	155
Mice	13.9	50	-	-	10.6	38
Fruits	-	-	40.3	145	-	-
Leaves	-	-	13.9	50	-	-
Unid.	8.3	30	-	-	-	-

   (b) Pie graphs: *See the next page of graph solutions.*

Drawing bar graphs:

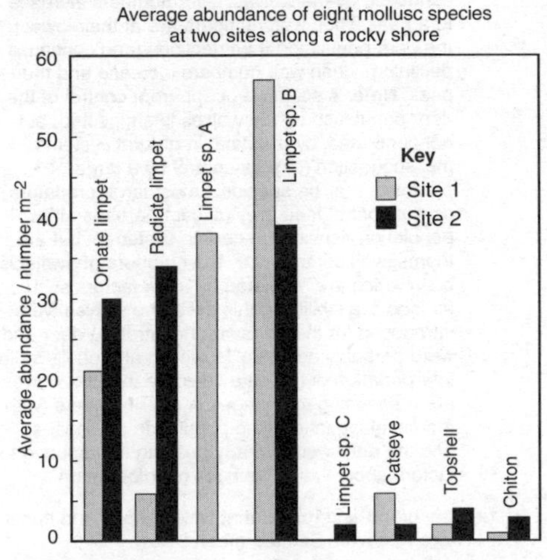

Drawing histograms:

Drawing pie graphs:

Key to food items in the diet

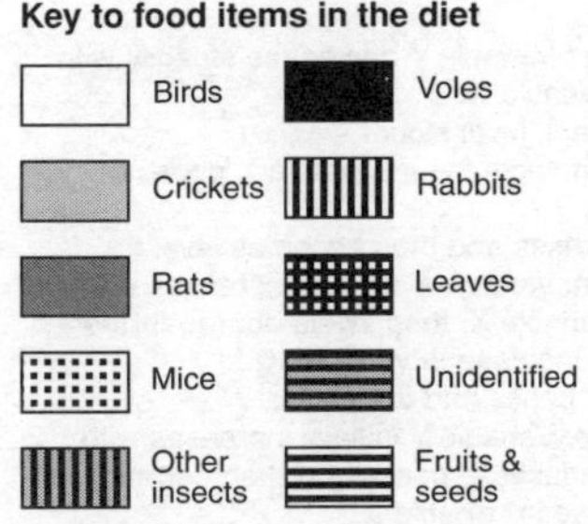

Percentage occurrence of different food items in the diets of stoats, rats, and cats

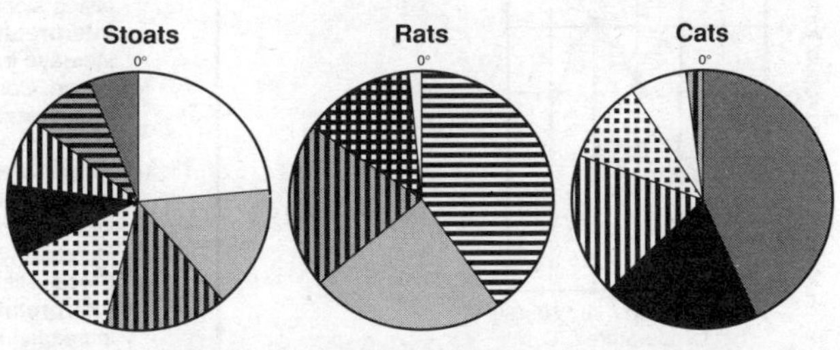

Drawing kite graphs:

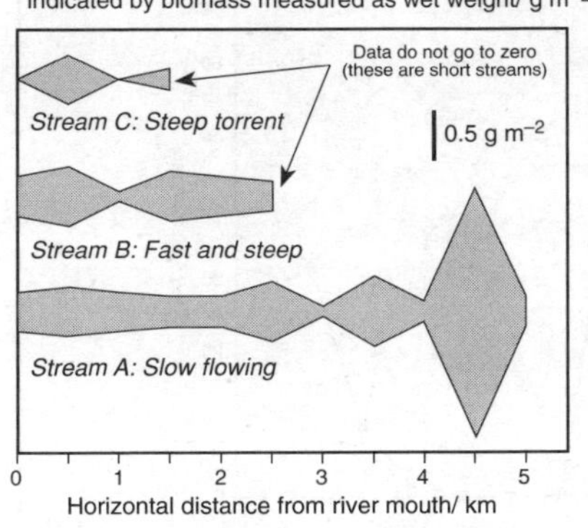

Drawing line graphs: Plotting multiple data sets

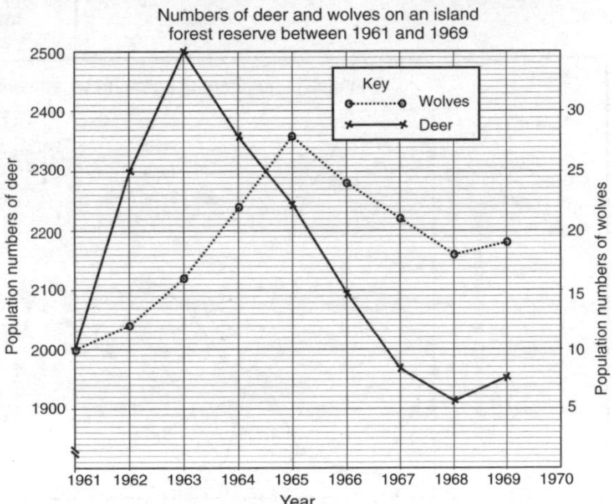

Drawing Kite Graphs (page 23)

1. (a) Table:

Distance from mouth/ *km*	Wet weight/ *g m⁻²*		
	Stm A	Stm B	Stm C
0	0.4	0.4	0
0.5	0.5	0.6	0.5
1.0	0.4	0.1	0
1.5	0.3	0.5	0.2
2.0	0.3	0.4	-
2.5	0.6	0.3	-
3.0	0.1	-	-
3.5	0.7	-	-
4.0	0.2	-	-
4.5	2.5	-	-
5.0	0.3	-	-

(b) Kite graph: *See previous page of graph solutions.*

Drawing Line Graphs (page 24)

1. (a) Line graph:

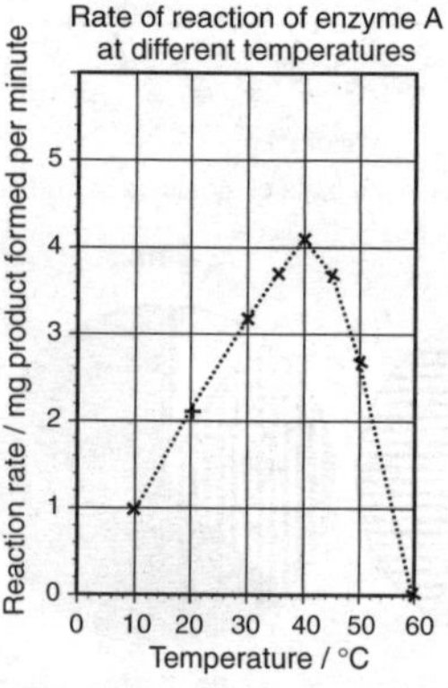

(b) Rate of reaction at 15°C = 1.6 mg product min⁻¹

2. (a) Line graph: See previous page of graph solutions.

(b) The data suggest that the deer population is being controlled by the wolves. Deer numbers increase to a peak when wolf numbers are at their lowest; the deer population then declines (and continues declining) when wolf numbers increase and then peak. **Note**: A scenario of apparent control of the deer population by the wolves is suggested, but not confirmed, by the data. In natural systems, this suggestion (of prey control by a large predator) *may* be specious; most large predators do not control their prey (except perhaps at low population densities in certain systems), but are themselves controlled by the numbers of available prey, which are regulated by other factors such as food availability. In this case, the wolves were introduced for the purpose of controlling deer and were probably doing so. However, an equally valid interpretation of the data could be that the wolves are responding to changes in deer numbers (with the usual lag inherent in population responses), and the deer were already peaking in response to factors about which we have no information.

3. (a) Line graph and (b) point at which shags and nests were removed: See the graph below.

Interpreting Line & Scatter Graphs (page 27)

1. (b) **Slope**: Negative linear relationship, with constantly falling slope.
   Interpretation: Variable Y decreases steadily with increase in variable X.

(c) **Slope**: Constant, level slope.
   Interpretation: Increase in variable X does not affect variable Y.

(d) **Slope**: Slope rises and then becomes level.
   Interpretation: Variable Y initially increases with increase in variable X, then levels out (no further increase with increase in variable X).

(e) **Slope**: Rises, peaks and then falls.
   Interpretation: Variable Y initially increases with increase in variable X, peaks and then declines with further increase in variable X.

(f) **Slope**: Exponentially increasing slope.
   Interpretation: As variable X increases, variable Y

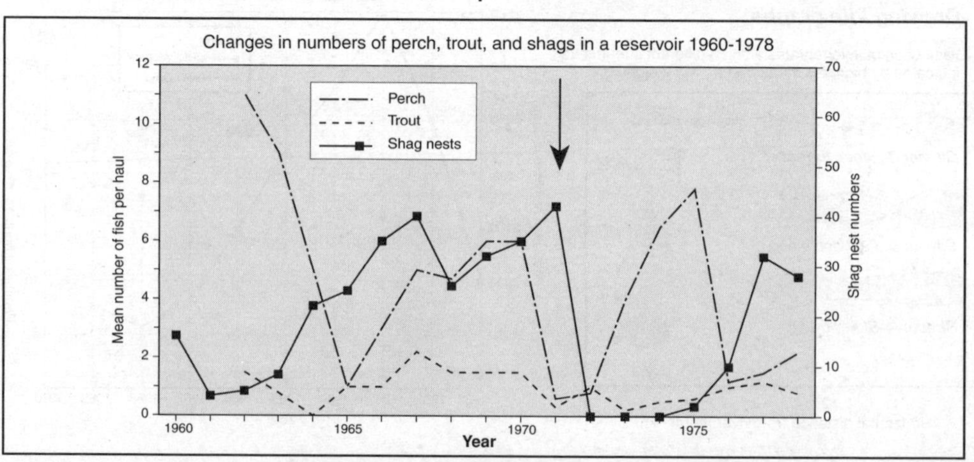

increases exponentially.

2. (a) Perch population fluctuations follow shag population fluctuations closely.
   (b) The evidence suggests that the fluctuations of shag and trout numbers are not related as the height of trout fluctuations in 1967 is reached before that of shag numbers.

Drawing Scatter Plots (page 28)

1. (a) Scatter plot and (b) Line of best fit:

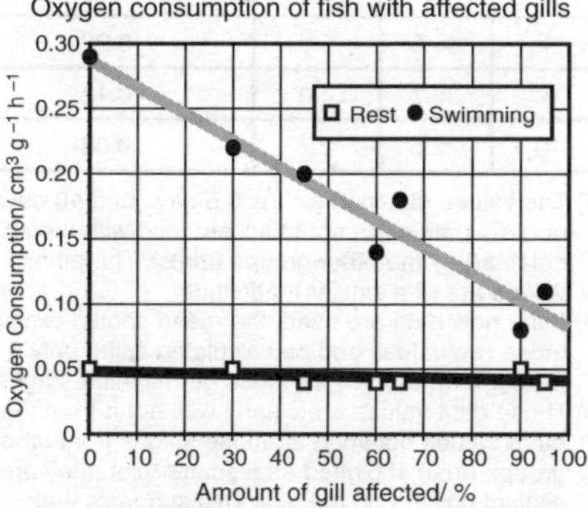

2. (a) At rest: No clear relationship; the line on the graph appears to have no significant slope (although this could be tested). **Note:** There is a slight tendency for oxygen consumption to fall as more of the gill becomes affected, but the scatter of points precludes making any conclusions about this.
   (b) Swimming: A negative linear relationship; the greater the proportion of affected gill, the lower the oxygen consumption.

3. The gill disease appears to have little or no effect on the oxygen uptake in resting fish.

Biological Drawings (page 29)

1. (a)-(h) any eight features in any order:
   - Lines cross over each other and are angled.
   - Cells are inaccurately drawn: they are not closed shapes, they do not even nearly represent what is actually there, there are overlaps.
   - There is no magnification given.
   - Drawing is cramped at the top corner of the page.
   - Labels are drawn on an angle.
   - There is no indication of whether the section is a cross section or longitudinal section.
   - There is a line to a cell type that has no label
   - Shading is inappropriate and does not indicate anything. It is apparently random and is unnecessary.
   - The material being drawn has not been identified accurately in the title by species.

2. Student's response required here. Some desirable features are shown in the figure on the top of the next column, but page position and size cannot be shown.

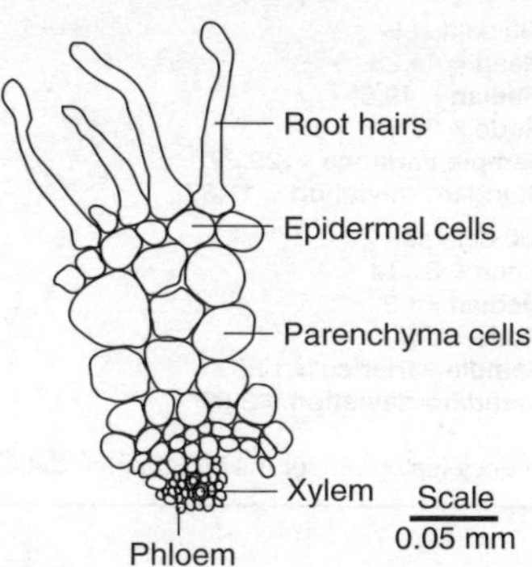

Root tranverse section from Ranunculus

3. A **biological drawing** is designed to convey useful information about the structure of an organism. From such diagrams another person should be able to clearly identify similar organisms and structures. By contrast, **artistic drawings** exhibit 'artistic licence' where the image is a single person's impression of what they saw. It may not be a reliable source of visual information about the structure of the organism.

Descriptive Statistics (page 31)

1. The modal value and associated ranked entries indicate that the variable being measured (spores per frond) has a bimodal distribution i.e. the data are not normally distributed. (Therefore) the mean and median are not accurate indicators of central tendency. Note also that the median differs from the mean; also an indication of a skewed (non-normal) distribution.

2. See results below:

Beetle mass /g	Tally	Total
2.1	|	1
2.2	||	2
2.4	|\	2
2.5	////|	4
2.6	//|	3
2.7	|	1
2.8	|\	2

Median = 8th value when in rank order = 2.5

Mode = 2.5

Mean = 2.49 ~ 2.5

Interpreting Sample Variability (page 33)

1. (a) 496/689 values within ± 1sd of the mean = 72% (48±7.8, i.e. between 40.2 and 55.8)
   (b) 671//689 values within ± 2 sd of the mean = 97% (48± 15.6, i.e. between 32.4 and 63.6)
   (c) The data are very close to being normally distributed about the mean (normal distribution + 67% of values lie within 1sd of the mean and 95% of values lie between 2 sd of the mean).

2. The mean and the median are very close.

3. N = 30 data set
   (a) **Mean** = 49.23
   (b) **Median** = 49.5
   (c) **Mode** = 38
   (d) **Sample variance** = 129.22
   (e) **Standard deviation** = 11.37

4. N = 50 data set
   (a) **Mean** = 61.44
   (b) **Median** = 63
   (c) **Mode** = 64
   (d) **Sample variance** = 14.59
   (e) **Standard deviation** = 3.82

5. Frequency histogram for the N=50 perch data set.

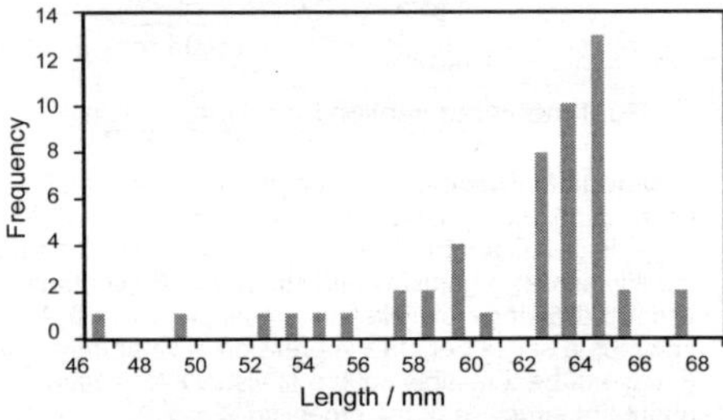

Frequency histogram for the N = 30 perch data set.

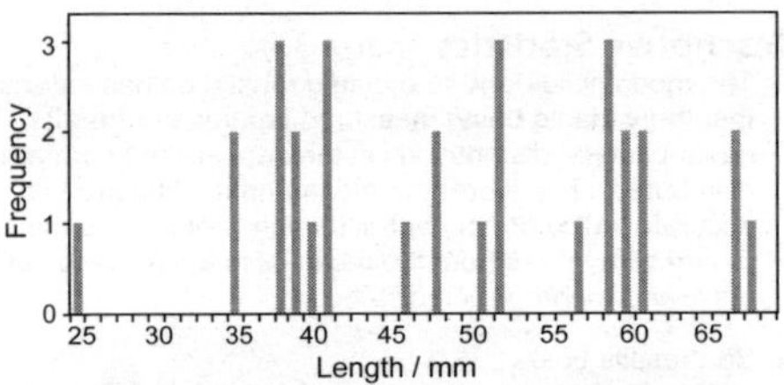

6. (a) The mean and median are very close to each other
       for the N=30 data set. There is a larger difference
       between the mean and median values obtained in
       the N=50 data set.
   (b) The standard deviation obtained for the N=30 set is
       much larger (11.37) compared to only 3.82 for the
       larger N=50 data set.
   (c) The N=30 data set more closely resembles the
       complete data set. The mean and median are
       quite close to those of the original data set. The
       mean, median and mode for the N=50 data set
       are considerably higher than those statistics for
       the complete data set. The sample variance and
       standard deviation values for the complete data set
       fall between those of the two smaller data sets.

7. (a) The frequency histogram for the N=30 data set
       shows a relatively normal distribution of data. M-
       The frequency histogram for the N=50 data set
       shows a non-normal distribution which is skewed to
       the right (negative skew).
   (b) The person who collected the sample in the N=30
       data set used equipment and techniques designed
       to collect fish randomly. As a result, a normal
       distribution of fish sizes was obtained by their
       sampling methods. M- Fish collection for the N=50
       sample set was biased. The mesh size used did
       not retain smaller fish, so a larger proportion of

bigger fish were collected. When plotted, the data
presented as a negative skew.

Evaluating Your Results (page 35)

1. $H_2O_2 \rightarrow H_2 + O_2$

2. (a)-(c), completed table for mean, stanadrd deviation,
   and rate below.

Stage	Mean	Std Dev	Mean rate / $cm^3\ s^{-1}\ g^{-1}$
0.5	10.1	0.5	0.03
2	34.9	3.8	0.12
4	65.5	5.0	0.22
6	36.7	4.0	0.12
10	22.5	2.7	0.08

3. (a) The values obtained for the 0.5 days and 10 days
       of germination are not in accordance with those
       obtained by the other groups (trials). The other
       values are of a similar magnitude.
   (b) If the new data are used, the mean should exclude
       those two values and be calculated using only 5
       (rather than 6) trials for those germination stages.
   (c) These data values are clearly well adrift from the
       other values obtained for those stages from other
       groups (trial); if plotted as a scatter plot, they are
       distinct outliers on the plot. This suggests that
       something was wrong with either the measurement
       of the execution of the trial. It is reasonable
       therefore to exclude them from the analysis.

4.

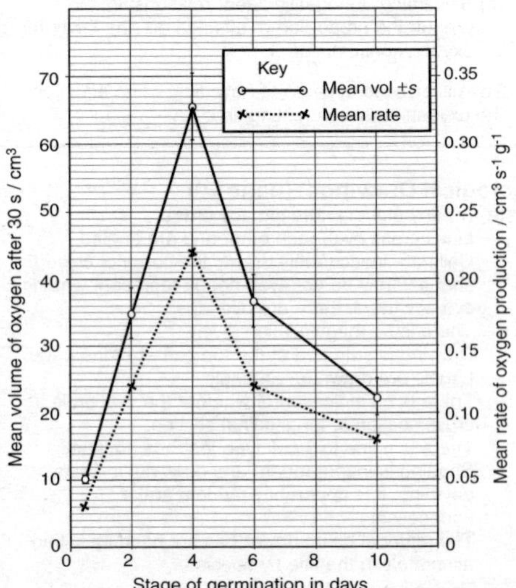

5. (a) The volume and rate of oxygen production increases
       rapidly to a peak at 4 days and declines, almost as
       sharply between 4 and 10 days.

(b) The catalase activity in the sprouting seeds increases rapidly in the first 4 days of germination linked to the increase in cell activity and high respiration rates in early growth. It then falls off as the seedlings become established and metabolism slows.

6. Errors include: The equipment could potentially leak around the bung or the tubing. There could be a delay in delivering all the H_2O_2 so a slight delay in correctly timing the start of the reaction. The seeds might not be completely crushed, or crushed to different degrees so that not all the catalase is released.

7. Validity of data could be affected by (two of): insufficient usable data, very variable data (overlapping data between times), old or poorly stored beans, old or poorly stored H_2O_2, precise and reliable data which was inaccurate because of gas losses through the equipment.

8. Improvements could include any one of: Using a mechanical grinder for a set period of time to ensure complete release of catalase. Using a petroleum sealant to prevent air leaks. Making sure the same person takes the measurement in each case, making sure all the trials are carried out with the same equipment by the same team.

KEY TERMS: Mix and Match (page 37)

Accuracy (O), Bibliography (Y), Biological drawing (C), Citation (A), Control (G), Controlled variable (K), Data (D), Datalogger (W), Dependent variable (I), Graph (R), Histogram (L), Hypothesis (M), Independent variable (B), Mean (H), Measurement (P), Median (N), Mode (E), Observation (S), Parameter (BB), Precision (Z), Qualitative data (U), Quantitative data (J), Raw data (Q), Reliability (X), Sample (V), Scientific method (T), Trend (of data) (F), Variable (AA)

The Causes of Disease (page 39)

1. An organism has a number of regions where its tissues interface with the environment; the skin, the respiratory system, the gut, and the urinogenital tract. These regions represent places where the body's tissues are in contact with the environment and where pathogens can invade the host more easily and gain entry to vulnerable tissues. For example, pathogenic microbes (cold virus, *Influenzavirus*, *M. tuberculosis*) can enter respiratory passages and penetrate gas exchange surfaces, *Vibrio cholerae* bacterium can be ingested with contaminated food or water and penetrate the defences of the gut epithelium, causing a change in ion transort and diarrhoea, vectors for pathogens (such as mosquitoes) can penetrate the skin's surface providing a way in which a pathogen (e.g. *Plasmodium*) can enter host tissues.

2. Multiple risk factors can work together to markedly increase the risk of developing a disease. In the case of cardiovascular disease, having any one of three risk factors (high blood lipids, glucose intolerance, or hypertension) increases risk of CVD by 1.5 to 2.3 times the level of risk of someone without those risk factors. When two of these risk factors are present, the risk level increases to 2.8-4X. When all three risk factors are present, the risk of developing the disease increases to over 6X. Multiple risk factors are commonly associated because the same dietary/lifestyle factors often contribute to different risk factors (e.g. hypertension, high blood lipids, and glucose intolerance are all associated with another risk factor - obesity). Smoking increases risk in these patients too because of its effects on the cardiovascular system.

Monosaccharides and Disaccharides (page 42)

1. (a) Primary energy source for cellular metabolism
   (b) Structural units for disaccharides and polysaccharides (food sources and structural carbohydrates).

2. (a) Lactose
   Enzyme: lactase
   Products: glucose and galactose
   Found: In the small intestine of mammals (secreted by the intestinal epithelial cells)
   (b) Maltose
   Enzyme: maltase
   Products: glucose monomers
   Found: In the intestine of animals (secreted by the intestinal epithelial cells), in germinating seeds. It is also found in bacteria and yeasts.
   (c) Sucrose
   Enzyme: sucrase or invertase
   Products: glucose and fructose
   Found: Sucrase is found in the small intestine of mammals (secreted by the intestinal epithelial cells). Invertase is found in plants and yeasts, and is also produced by honeybees. Note invertase and sucrase both hydrolyse sucrose but by different mechanisms: Invertases cleave the O-C(fructose) bond, whereas the sucrases cleave the O-C(glucose) bond

3. A lactose intolerance would arise when a person fails to produce lactase in the small intestine and so cannot metabolise lactose, which passes into the colon uncleaved (bacterial utilisation of this substrate in the colon causes the intestinal symptoms of the intolerance). **Extra note**: Lactase production naturally declines in adulthood, but a mutation on chromosome 2 prevents this lactase shutdown and enables utilisation of lactose throughout adult life. This mutation has arisen independently in northern Europe and east Africa and appears to be an evolutionarily recent adaptation to dairy consumption.

Carbohydrate Chemistry (page 43)

1. **Structural isomers** have the same molecular formula but their atoms are linked in different sequences. For example, fructose and glucose are structural isomers because, although they have the same molecular formula ($C_6H_{12}O_6$), glucose contains an aldehyde group (it is an aldose) and fructose contains a keto group (it is a ketose). In contrast, **optical isomers** are identical in every way except that they are mirror images of each other. The two ring forms of glucose, α and β glucose, are optical isomers, being two mirror image forms.

2. Compound sugars are formed and broken down by condensation and hydrolysis reactions respectively. **Condensation reactions** join two carbohydrate molecules by a glycosidic bond with the release of a water molecule. **Hydrolysis reactions** use water to split a carbohydrate molecule into two, where the water molecule is used to provide a hydrogen atom and a hydroxyl group.

3. Isomers will have different bonding properties and will form different disaccharides and macromolecules depending on the isomer involved, e.g. glucose and fructose are structural isomers; glucose + glucose forms maltose, glucose + fructose from sucrose. A polysaccharide of the α isomer of glucose forms starch whereas the β isomer forms cellulose.

Polysaccharides (page 44)

1. Polysaccharides are a good source of energy because they are easily hydrolysed into monosaccharides (e.g. glucose) when energy is needed. Monosaccharides are the primary source of cellular fuel.

2. Cellulose, starch, and glycogen are all polymers of glucose, but differ in form and function because of the optical isomer involved, the length of the polymers, and the degree of branching. **Cellulose** is an unbranched, long chain glucose polymer held by β-1,4 glycosidic bonds. The straight, tightly packed chains give cellulose high tensile strength and resistance to hydrolysis. **Starch** is a mixture of two polysaccharides: amylose (unbranched with α-1,4 glycosidic bonds) and amylopectin (branched with α-1,6 glycosidic bonds). The α-1,4 glycosidic bonds and more branched nature of starch account for its physical properties; starch is powdery and more easily hydrolysed than cellulose, which exists as tough microfibrils. **Glycogen**, like starch, is a branched polymer. It is similar to amylopectin, being composed of α-glucose molecules, but it is larger and more there are more α-1,6 links. This makes it highly branched, more soluble, and more easily hydrolysed than starch.

Amino Acids (page 45)

1. Amino acids are the building blocks for constructing proteins (which have diverse structural and metabolic functions). Amino acids are also the precursors of many important molecules (e.g. neurotransmitters and hormones).

2. The side chains (R groups) differ in their chemical structure (and therefore their chemical effect).

3. Translation of the genetic code. Genetic instructions from the chromosomes (genes on the DNA) determine the order in which amino acids are joined together.

4. **Essential amino acids** cannot be manufactured by the human body, they must be included in the food we eat.

5. **Condensation reactions** involve the joining of two amino acids (or an amino acid to a dipeptide or polypeptide) by a peptide bond with the release of a water molecule.

6. **Hydrolysis** involves the splitting of a dipeptide (or the splitting of an amino acid from a polypeptide) where the peptide bond is broken and a water molecule is used to provide a hydrogen atom and a hydroxyl group.

7. The L-form.

Proteins (page 47)

1. (a) **Structural**: Proteins form an important component of connective tissues and epidermal structures: collagen, keratin (hair, horn etc.). Proteins are also found scattered on, in, and through cell membranes, but tend to have a regulatory role in this instance. Proteins are also important in maintaining a tightly coiled structure in a condensed chromosome.
   (b) **Regulatory**: **Hormones** such as insulin, adrenaline (modified amino acid), glucagon (peptide) are chemical messengers released from glands to trigger a response in a target tissue. They help maintain homeostasis. **Enzymes** regulate metabolic processes in cells.
   (c) **Contractile**: Actin and myosin are structural components of muscle fibres. Using a ratchet system, these two proteins move past each other when energy is supplied.
   (d) **Immunological**: Gamma globulins are blood proteins that act as antibodies, targeting antigens (foreign substances and microbes) for immobilisation and destruction.
   (e) **Transport**: Haemoglobin and myoglobin are proteins that act as carrier molecules for transporting oxygen in the bloodstream of vertebrates. Invertebrates usually have some other type of oxygen carrying molecule in the blood.
   (f) **Catalytic**: Enzymes, e.g. amylase, lipase, lactase, trypsin, are involved in the chemical digestion of food. A vast variety of other enzymes are involved in just about every metabolic process in organisms.

2. Denaturation destroys protein function because it involves an irreversible change in the precise tertiary or quaternary structure that confers biological activity. For example, a denatured enzyme protein may not have its reactive sites properly aligned, and will be prevented from attracting the substrate molecule.

3. Fibrous proteins have a tertiary structure that produces long fibers or sheets, often with many cross-linkages. This makes them very tough physically and ideal as structural molecules e.g. collagen.

4. The tertiary structure of globular proteins produces a spherical shape which is critical to their interaction with other molecules, e.g. the active site in enzymes or the recognition sites in regulatory molecules like insulin.

Enzymes (page 49)

1. The active site is the region where substrate is drawn in and positioned in such a way as to promote the reaction. The properties of the active site are a function of the precise configuration of the amino acid side chains which interact with the substrate.

2. A mutation could result in a different amino acid being positioned in the polypeptide chain. The final protein may be folded incorrectly (incorrect tertiary and quaternary structure) and lose its biological function. **Note**: If the mutation is silent or in a non-critical region of the enzyme, biological function may not be affected.

3. **Catabolism** involves metabolic reactions that break

large molecules into smaller ones. Such reactions include digestion and cellular respiration. They release energy and are therefore **exergonic**. In contrast, **anabolism** involves metabolic reactions that build larger molecules from smaller ones. Anabolic reactions include protein synthesis and photosynthesis. They require the input of energy and are **endergonic**.

How Enzymes Work (page 50)

1. Enzymes are biological molecules (usually proteins) that act as catalysts, allowing reactions to proceed more readily. They do this by influencing bond stability in the reactants and thereby lowering the activation energy required to create an unstable transition state in the substrate from which the reaction proceeds readily.

2. The **lock and key model** proposed that the substrate was simply drawn into a closely matching cleft (active site) on the enzyme. In this model, the enzyme's active site was a somewhat passive recipient of the substrate, whereas studies of enzyme inhibitors since showed that assumption to be incorrect.

3. The **induced fit model** is a modified version of the lock and key in which the substrate and the active site interact. Substrate binding causes the active site to change slightly so that bonds in the substrate(s) are destabilised. This model is supported by evidence from studies of enzyme inhibition.

Enzyme Reaction Rates (page 51)

1. (a) An increase in enzyme concentration increases reaction rate.
   (b) By manufacturing more or less (increasing or decreasing the rate of protein synthesis).

2. (a) An increase in **substrate concentration** increases reaction rate to a point. Reaction rate does not continue increasing but levels off as the amount of substrate continues to increase.
   (b) The reaction rate changes because after a certain substrate level the enzymes are fully saturated by substrate and the rate cannot increase any more.

3. (a) An optimum **temperature** for an enzyme is the temperature at which enzyme activity is maximum.
   (b) Most enzymes perform poorly at low temperatures because chemical reactions occur slowly or not all at low temperatures (enzyme activity will reappear when the temperature increases; usually enzymes are not damaged by moderately low temperatures).

4. (a) Optimum **pH**: Pepsin: 1-2, trypsin: approx. 7.5-8.2, urease: approx. 6.5-7.0
   (b) The stomach is an acidic environment which is the ideal pH for pepsin.

Enzyme Cofactors (page 52)

1. **Cofactors** are non-protein components that complete an enzyme, i.e. enable its functional catalytic activity.

2. Cofactors either complete the active site or make the active site more reactive (e.g. by facilitating the substrate-enzyme interaction).

3. The apoenzyme is the protein portion of the functionally active enzyme. The cofactor is the non-protein portion required to complete the enzyme's catalytic activity.

4. Two broad categories of cofactors are **organic cofactors**, such as vitamin C, and **inorganic ions** (such as Ca^{2+} and Zn^{2+})

5. Many vitamins and minerals are cofactors so an adequate dietary intake ensures that all necessary cofactors are present as required for enzyme function.

Enzyme Inhibitors (page 53)

1. In **competitive inhibition**, the inhibitor competes with the substrate for the enzyme's active site and, once in place, prevents substrate binding. A **noncompetitive inhibitor** does not occupy the active site but binds to some other part of the enzyme, making it less able to perform its function as an effective biological catalyst.

2. (a) With a competitive inhibitor present, the effect of the competition can be overcome by increasing the substrate concentration; the rate of the reaction will slow, but will eventually reach the same level as that achieved without an inhibitor. In a system where there is a non-competitive inhibitor, the rate of the reaction slows and is well below the maximum that can be achieved without an inhibitor. This rate depression cannot be overcome by increasing the substrate concentration.
   (b) Type of inhibition could be tested by increasing the substrate concentration. If this overcame the rate depression then the inhibition is competitive.

3. Noncompetitive inhibition is similar to allosteric inhibition in that they both involve the inhibitor binding at a site other than the active site, thereby changing the conformation of the active site and stopping the activity of the enzyme. However, allosteric inhibition is always reversible and a feature of regulation in metabolic pathways. Non-competitive inhibition may be irreversible, in which case the inhibitor is a poison.

4. Heavy metals are toxic because they bind to the active sites of enzymes and permanently inactivate them. While the active site is occupied by the heavy metal the enzyme is non-functional. Because they are lost exceedingly slowly from the body, anything other than a low level of these metals is toxic.

5. (a) Some antibiotics, such as penicillin, are irreversible inhibitors to the enzymes essential for wall synthesis in bacteria. Susceptible bacteria are unable to build cell walls after dividing so their growth is stopped.
   (b) Human cells do not have a cell wall and so they are unaffected by the enzyme inhibition.

The Mouth and Pharynx (page 55)

1. (a) To break down the food by chewing.
   (b) To lubricate the food and mix it with saliva to being the process of chemical digestion.

2. The epiglottis prevents food from going into the trachea and instead directs it to the esophagus. This can be inferred from its position and by the fact that it is normally pointed upward during breathing but is more horizontal during swallowing.

3. Tonsils provide immune protection against pharyngeal and upper respiratory tract infections.

The Human Digestive Tract (page 56)

1. Structures as follows:

   A Mouth and teeth   G Gall bladder
   B Salivary glands   H Colon (or large intestine)
   C Esophagus   I Small intestine
   D Liver   J Rectum
   E Stomach   K Appendix
   F Pancreas   L Anus

   Region responsible for each stated function as follows:
   (a) I - small intestine   (e) F - pancreas (or B)
   (b) J - rectum   (f) D - liver
   (c) H - colon   (g) B - salivary gland
   (d) E - stomach

2. Position of sphincters below.

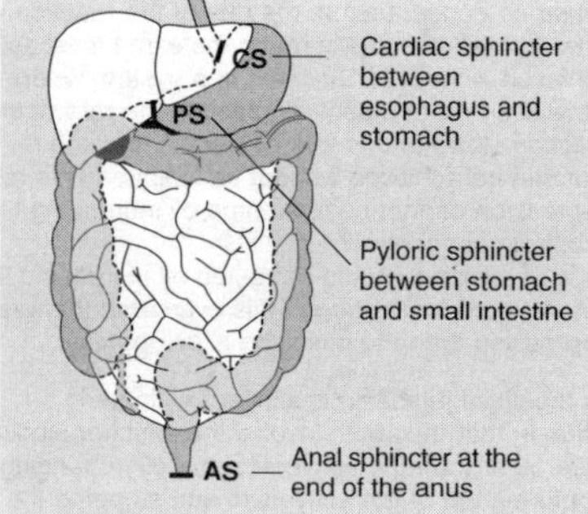

3. (a) Lining (mucosa) of the stomach.
       Features: gastric gland.
   (b) Villi lining lumen of the small intestine (duodenum).
       Feature: Fingerlike villi project into the lumen. Layer of muscle visible below connective tissue of villi.
   (c) Liver. Feature: Bile ducts.

4. (a) Stomach: A three layered muscular wall to produce the movements to mix the food into chyme. Rugae allow expansion of volume. gastric glands specialised to produce acid, mucus, and pepsinogen (activated in acid to protein-digesting pepsin).
   (b) Small intestine: Fingerlike villi project into the lumen and provide large surface area for absorption of nutrients. Intestinal glands produce mucus to protect gut mucosa from damage and alkaline fluid to provide an appropriate pH for intestinal and pancreatic enzymes.
   (c) Large intestine: Simple columnar epithelium absorbs water from the slurry. Epithelium has many tubular glands which produce mucus to lubricate colon walls and aid faeces formation. Strong muscular walls move material through the colon.

5. (a) and (b): any two of the following in any order:
   Site: Stomach   *Enzyme*: pepsin
   Purpose: Digestion of proteins to polypeptides.

   Site: Pancreas   *Enzyme*: pancreatic amylase
   Purpose: Digestion of starch to maltose.

   Site: Pancreas   *Enzymes*: trypsin/chymotrypsin
   Purpose: Digestion of proteins to polypeptides.

   Site: Pancreas   *Enzyme*: pancreatic lipase
   Purpose: Digestion of fats to fatty acids and glycerol.

   Site: Pancreas   *Enzymes*: peptidases
   Purpose: Digestion of polypeptides to amino acids.

   Site: Intestinal mucosa *Enzymes*: peptidases.
   Purpose: Digestion of polypeptides to amino acids.

   Site: Intestinal mucosa *Enzymes*: maltase, lactase, sucrase
   Purpose: Digestion of carbohydrates (maltose, lactose, sucrose respectively) into their constituent parts.

6. (a) The enzymes involved in digestion in different regions of the gut have specific **pH optima** (pH at which they operate most efficiently), so secretions are regionally pH appropriate. **Note**: For pepsin (stomach) this optimum is acid pH 1.5-2.0, for the enzymes in the small intestine, the optimum is alkaline pH 7.5-8.2.
   (b) The enzymes are secreted as inactive precursors in order to prevent their activity in the site of production and release (where they would damage the tissue). Once in the gut lumen, they can be activated to digest the food (the gut lining itself is protected by mucus).

7. (a) Food is moved through the gut by perstalsis (wave like contractions of smooth muscle).
   (b) Sphincters regulate the passage of food through the gut, allowing material to pass more quickly through the gut, or holding it back. Their activity depends on speed of digestion, food type, the influence of hormones, and the fullness of the gut.
   Note: Sphincter contraction partly or completely closes an orifice.

8. (a) Passage too rapid: Too little water is reabsorbed leading to diarrhea.
   (b) Passage too slow: Too much water is reabsorbed leading to compaction of faeces and constipation.

Digestion, Absorption, and Transport (page 59)

1. Amylase breaks down the amylose present in starch into the disaccharide maltose and short chain carbohydrates such as dextrose. Maltase is required to separate the glucose monomers making up maltose and dextrose into the glucose monomers and thus allow absorption by the intestinal cells.

2. Digesting starch allows humans to gain glucose for energy from a wider range of foods such as grains and tubers (such as potatoes) which store sugars as starch. This means the reliance of fruits for glucose is reduced.

3. Lactase allows the sugars in breast milk to be digested by an infant, thus allowing the gain of the energy they require. In adults it continues this purpose, but also allows an easy way of obtaining calcium by allowing milk to be digested without side effects.

4. (a) Glucose and galactose: Active transport.
   (b) Fructose: diffusion.
   (c) Amino acids: Active transport.
   (d) Dipeptides: Active transport.
   (e) Tripeptides: Active transport.

(f) Short chain fatty acids: Diffusion.
(g) Monoglycerides: Diffusion.
(h) Fat soluble vitamins: Diffusion.

3. In mammals, the lining of the gut is folded into a system of finger-like villi, which increase gut surface area. This increases the area over which nutrients can be taken up which speeds up absorption and (in normal circumstances) leads to increased assimilation rates.

Biochemical Tests (page 61)

1. Lipids are insoluble in water. They will not form an emulsion in water unless they have first been dissolved in ethanol (a non-polar solvent).

2. (a) To quantify the glucose concentration of commercial drinks, you would (1) perform a Benedict's test on each of the unknown drinks (dilute if necessary), (2) measure the absorbance value of the colour change, (3) use the calibration curve prepared from a series of know glucose standards to read off the glucose concentration of the unknowns.
   (b) You would have to dilute the drinks so their concentrations fell within the range of the calibration curve.

3. The acidic conditions break the glycosidic bond in a non-reducing sugar (e.g sucrose) through hydrolysis. The products of decomposition (e.g. of sucrose) are monosaccharides (e.g. glucose and fructose), both of which can be detected by Benedict's reagent.

4. Lipids are insoluble in water. They will not form an emulsion in water unless they have first been dissolved in ethanol (a non-polar solvent).

KEY TERMS: Word Find (page 62)

```
P U K G T T E R T I A R Y S T R U C T U R E P O F
H E N Y N M X A S E P E N Z Y M E S P O U Q K C D
Q J P K Q L Y A V I L L I C O N D E N S A T I O N
R X F T P R I M A R Y S T R U C T U R E A Y K D S
A S L H I H Y D R O L Y S I S Z I M C D H A Q E A
B D M W P D E L E X E R G O N I C Q M E C T T N N
S P V A L B E R K O M J C O L O R I M E T R Y A G
O A A O L M O S Y S A C T I V E S I T E T N X T L
R N S A L L O S T E R I C I N H I B I T O R S U Y
P C V T O S I F U A M I N O A C I D S T Y G S R C
T R G Q D L U N G N X R Q G L Y C O S I D I C A O
I E L S D W D B T N Q A H E B I L E S A L T S T G
O A E U N C V K X E M W E U O A S T A R C H Q I E
N S A B I S O M E R S Q Y C X C P S K J S I I O N
V H U A M Y L A S E M T Q P E P S I N N G Y C N J
C O F A C T O R S N S T I Q B W D I P E P T I D E
D H Y A N A B O L I C F D N U Z K W S K T T K O Z
G I N D U C E D F I T P B I E C E L L U L O S E C
```

Eukaryotic Cell Diversity (page 64)

1. (a) **Plant cells**: Mesophyll cell, vessel element (note that this is a dead cell), guard cells.
   (b) **Characteristics**: Cellulose cell wall, chloroplasts containing the photosynthetic pigments chlorophyll *a* and *b*, carbohydrate stored as starch, large vacuoles.

2. (a) **Animal cells**: Osteocyte, leucocyte, smooth muscle cell, epidermal cells of skin, neurone, erythrocyte.

(b) **Characteristics**: No cellulose cell wall, no chloroplasts or plastids of any kind, vacuoles if present are small, no regular geometric shape.

3. (a) **Protoctistans**: *Amoeba, Euglena, Paramecium, Spirogyra, Chlamydomonas*.
   (b) **Characteristics**: A very diverse group (the eukaryotes that do not fit into plant, animal, or fungi classification). Generally refers to unicellular eukaryotes, although some primitive multicellular organisms have been included in recent years. Includes protozoans which are heterotrophic (animal-like in their nutrition), and algae, which have chloroplasts and are autotrophic (plant-like in their nutrition). A difficult group to give general characteristics for because they are so diverse. Often ciliated (e.g. *Paramecium*) or flagellated (e.g. *Euglena*). Note that the cyanobacteria are now classified within Prokaryotae (not Protoctista).

4. (a) **Fungal cells**: Yeast, pin mould hyphae.
   (b) **Characteristics**: Eukaryotes, usually multicellular, all are heterotrophs (no photosynthetic ability), lack chloroplasts. Except in yeasts, the basic fungus body is composed of basic building blocks called hyphae. Cell walls composed mainly of chitin.

Animal Cells (page 65)

1. The many tiny infoldings of the intestinal microvilli provide a very large surface area over which nutrients can be absorbed. This speeds up the processing of food, which is an essential feature of providing for high energy demands.

2. (a) Intestinal epithelium: The mucus secreting cells here are the **goblet cells**. They secrete mucus to protect the epithelium from abrasion and from the action of the enzymes involved in digesting the food.
   (b) Stomach: The mucus secreting cells here are the **mucous cells**. Their secretions protect the stomach epithelium from the highly acidic, protein digesting environment.

3. The stomach lining is pitted with gastric glands, which contain the specialised cells (mucous cells, parietal cells, and chief cells) to secrete mucus, acid, and an enzyme precursor, pepsinogen. Although the stomach has folds, or rugae, to accommodate expansion of volume, its surface is not so greatly infolded as that of the small intestine, where the epithelium is pushed up into villi, and each villus has many fingerlike protrusions (microvilli) that project into the intestinal lumen. The intestinal glands lie between the villi, and secrete mucus (from goblet cells) and an alkaline fluid. The enzymes secreted by the intestinal epithelium are bound to the surfaces of the epithelial cells.

4. A: Neurone: Specialised for the generation and maintenance of electrical impulses. Long extensions of the cell body carry electrical impulses towards connections with other cells.
   B: White blood cell: Large cells, some are mobile and capable of phagocytosis, others produce substances such as histamine or antibodies, which are involved in the body's defence responses.
   C: Red blood cell: Small cells, lacking nuclei and packed with haemoglobin, which binds oxygen and

transports it around the body. Relatively short lived cells with a rapid turnover.

Cell Sizes (page 67)

1.
(a) *Amoeba*:	300 µm	0.3 mm
(b) Foraminiferan:	400 µm	0.4 mm
(c) *Leptospira*:	7-8 µm	0.007-0.008 mm
(d) Epidermis:	120 µm	0.12 mm
(e) *Daphnia*:	2500 µm	2.5 mm
(f) *Papillomavirus*:	0.13 µm	0.00013 mm

2. *Papillomavirus*; *Leptospira*; Epidermis (but not an organism); *Amoeba*; Foraminiferan; *Daphnia*

3. Onion epidermis (possibly); *Amoeba*; foraminiferan; *Daphnia*

4. (a) 0.00025 mm   (b) 0.45 mm   (c) 0.0002 mm

The Cell's Cytoskeleton (page 68)

1. All components of the cytoskeleton are made up of protein subunits.

2. The dynamic nature is important because it enables movement of the cell itself and of materials in the cell, while resisting tension and providing structural support.

3. Cytoskeletal elements (microtubules and microfilaments) act as railroad tracks along which vesicles and organelles can move to specific places. This is an active process and carried out by motor proteins in the cell, which attach to the cytoskeletal elements and 'walk' materials along them.

Cell Structures and Organelles (page 69)

(b) **Name**: Ribosome
Location: Free in cytoplasm or bound to rough ER
Function: Synthesize polypeptides (=proteins)
Present in plant cells: Yes
Present in animal cells: Yes
Visible under LM: No

(c) **Name**: Mitochondrion
Location: In cytoplasm as discrete organelles
Function: Site of cellular respiration (ATP formation)
Present in plant cells: Yes
Present in animal cells: Yes
Visible under LM: Not with most standard school LM, but can be seen using high quality, high power LM.

(d) **Name**: Golgi apparatus
Location: In cytoplasm associated with the smooth endoplasmic reticulum, often close to the nucleus.
Function: Final modification of proteins and lipids. Sorting and storage for use in the cell or packaging molecules for export.
Present in plant cells: Yes
Present in animal cells: Yes
Visible under LM: Not with most standard school LM, but may be visible using high quality, high power LM.

(e) **Name**: Endoplasmic reticulum (in this case, rough ER)
Location: Penetrates the whole cytoplasm
Function: Involved in the transport of materials (e.g. proteins) within the cell and between the cell and its surroundings.
Present in plant cells: Yes
Present in animal cells: Yes

Visible under LM: No

(f) **Name**: Cytoskeleton
Location: Throughout cytoplasm
Function: Provides structure and shape to a cell, responsible for cell movement (e.g. during muscle contraction), and provides intracellular transport of organelles and other structures.
Present in plant cells: Yes
Present in animal cells: Yes
Visible under LM: No

(g) **Name**: Lysosome and food vaculoe (given)
Lysosome
Location: Free in cytoplasm.
Function: Ingests and destroys foreign material. Able to digest the cell itself under some circumstances.
Present in plant cells: Yes but variably (vacuoles may have a lysosomal function in some plant cells).
Present in animal cells: Yes
Visible under LM: No

Vacuole (a food vacuole in an animal cell is shown, so students may answer with respect to this).
Location: In cytoplasm.
Function: In plant cells, the vacuole (often only one) is a large fluid filled structure involved in storage and support (turgor). In animal cells, vacuoles are smaller and more numerous, and are involved in storage (of water, wastes, and soluble pigments).
Present in plant cells: Yes, as (a) large structure(s).
Present in animal cells: Yes, smaller, more numerous
Visible under LM: Yes in plant cells, no in animal cells.

(h) **Name**: Nucleus
Location: Discrete organelle, position is variable.
Function: The control center of the cell; the site of the nuclear material (DNA).
Present in plant cells: Yes
Present in animal cells: Yes
Visible under LM: Yes.

(i) **Name**: Centrioles
Location: In cytoplasm, usually next to the nucleus.
Function: Involved in cell division (probably in the organisation of the spindle fibers).
Present in plant cells: Variably (absent in higher plants)
Present in animal cells: Yes
Visible under LM: No.

(j) **Name**: Cilia and flagella (given)
Location: Anchored in the cell membrane and extending outside the cell.
Function: Motility.
Present in plant cells: No
Present in animal cells: Yes
Visible under LM: Variably (depends on magnification and preparation/fixation of material).

Prokaryotic Cells (page 71)

1. (a) The nuclear material (DNA) is not contained within a clearly defined nucleus with a nuclear membrane.
   (b) Membrane-bound cellular organelles (e.g. mitochondria, endoplasmic reticulum) are missing.
   (c) Single, circular chromosome sometimes with accessory chromosomes called plasmids.

2. (a) Locomotion: Flagella enable bacterial movement out of unsuitable conditions to preferred conditions.
   (b) Fimbriae are shorter, straighter, and thinner than flagella. Used for attachment rather than locomotion.

3. (a) Bacterial cell wall lies outside the plasma (cell surface) membrane. It is a semi-rigid structure composed of a macromolecule called peptidoglycan, and contains varying amounts of lipopolysacchardies and lipoproteins.
   (b) The glycocalyx is a viscous, gelatinous layer which lies outside the cell wall. It usually comprises polysaccharide and/or polypeptide, but not peptidoglycan, and may be firmly or loosely attached to the wall.

4. (a) Bacteria usually reproduce by binary fission, where the DNA replicates and the cell then splits into two.
   (b) Conjugation differs from binary fission in that DNA is exchanged between one bacterial cell (the donor) and another (the recipient). The recipient cell gains DNA from the donor.

5. A number of features contribute to the ability of bacteria to causes disease, although not all bacteria possess all features. These include:
   - Rapid rates of growth and division in the right environment, which speeds up invasion of the host's tissues and means that evolutionary changes affecting virulence occur rapidly)
   - An ability to acquire genes affecting virulence through conjugation (horizontal evolution). – Ability to form resistant endospores which remain viable to reinfect a host at a later stage.
   - Glycocalyx (capsules and slime layers) enables attachment to host tissues, contributes to virulence, and can protect from host immune defences.

Optical Microscopes (page 73)

1. (a) Eyepiece lens
   (b) Arm
   (c) Coarse focus knob
   (d) Fine focus knob
   (e) Objective lens
   (f) Mechanical stage
   (g) Condenser
   (h) In-built light source
   (i) Eyepiece lens
   (j) Eyepiece focus
   (k) Focus knob
   (l) Objective lens
   (m) Stage

2. Phase contrast is used where the specimen is transparent to increase contrast between structures. **Note**: It is superior to dark field because a better image of the interior of specimens is obtained.

3. (a) Plant cell, any two of: Cell wall, nucleus (may see chromatin if stained appropriately), vacuole, cell membrane (high magnification), Golgi apparatus, mitochondria (high magnification), chloroplast, cytoplasm (if stained), nuclear envelope (maybe).
   (b) Animal cell, any two of: Nucleus (may see chromatin if stained appropriately), centriole, cell membrane (high magnification), Golgi apparatus, mitochondria (high magnification), cytoplasm (if stained).

4. Any of: Ribosomes, microtubules, endoplasmic reticulum, Golgi vesicles (free), nuclear envelope as two layers, lysosomes (animal cells). Also detail of organelles such as mitochondria and chloroplasts.

5. (a) Leishman's stain
   (b) Schultz's solution/iodine solution
   (c) Schultz's solution
   (d) Aniline sulfate/ Schultz's solution
   (e) Methylene blue
   (f) Schultz's solution

6. (a) 600X magnification   (b) 600X magnification

7. Bright field, compound light microscopes produce a flat (2-dimensional) image from a thin, transparent sample. Dissecting microscopes produce a 3-dimensional image, revealing the surface details of the specimen.

8. Magnification is the number of times larger an image is than the specimen. Resolution is the degree of achievable detail. The limit of resolution is the minimum distance by which two points in a specimen can be separated and still be distinguished as separate points. **Note**: By adding stronger, or more, lenses, a LM can magnify an image many 1000s of times but its resolution is limited. EMs have greater resolving power because of the very short wavelength of the electrons.

Electron Microscopes (page 75)

1. The limit of resolution (see #8 above) is related to wavelength (about 0.45X the wavelength). The shortest visible light has a wavelength of about 450 nm giving a resolution of 0.45 x 450 nm; close to 200 nm. Points less than 200 nm apart will be perceived as one point or a blur. Electron beams have a shorter wavelength than light so the resolution is much greater (points 0.5 nm apart can be distinguished as separate points; a resolving power that is 400X that of a light microscope).

2. (a) **TEM**: Used to (any of): show cell ultrastructure i.e. organelles; to investigate changes in the number, size, shape, or condition of cells and organelles i.e. demonstrate cellular processes or activities; to detect the presence of viruses in cells.
   (b) **SEM**: Used to (any of): show the surface features of cells, e.g. guard cell surrounding a stoma; to show the surface features of organisms for identification (often used for invertebrates and viruses); for general identification by surface feature, e.g. for pollen used in palaeoclimate or forensic research.
   (c) **Bright field**: Used for (any of): examining prepared sections of tissue for cellular detail; for examining living tissue for large scale movements, e.g. blood flow in capillaries or cytoplasmic streaming.
   (d) **Dissecting**: Used for (any of): examining living specimens for surface detail and structures; sorting material from samples (e.g. leaf litter or stream invertebrates; dissecting a small organism where greater resolution than the naked eye is required.

3.
A TEM	E SEM
B Bright field LM	F Bright field LM
C TEM	G Dissecting LM
D Bright field LM	H SEM

Cell Fractionation (page 77)

1. Cell organelles have different densities and spin down at different rates. Smaller organelles take longer to spin down and require a higher centrifugation speed to separate out.

2. The sample is homogenized (broken up) before centrifugation to rupture the cell surface membrane, break open the cell, and release the cell contents.

3. (a) Isotonic solution is needed so that there are no volume changes in the organelles.
   (b) Cool solution prevent self digestion of the organelles

by enzymes released during homogenization.
(c) Buffered solution prevents pH changes that might denature enzymes and other proteins.

4. (a) Ribosomes and endoplasmic reticulum
   (b) Lysosomes and mitochondria
   (c) Nuclei

Identifying Structures in an Animal Cell
(page 78)

1. (a) Plasma membrane   (e) Lysosome
   (b) Rough ER   (f) Nucleus
   (c) Centriole (TS)   (g) Golgi aparatus
   (d) Mitochondrion   (h) Cytoplasm

2. Centrioles

3. Plant cells are enclosed by a rigid cellulose cell wall and do not have the capacity for motility or phagocytosis in the way that animal cells do.

4. (a) High protein production and secretion indicated by a relatively large amount of ER and an extensive Golgi apparatus.
   (b) Large number of mitochondria indicate that it is metabolically very active (high respiration rate).

5. It has a membrane-bound nucleus and membrane-bound organelles.

Identifying Plant Cell Structures (page 79)

1. (a) Cytoplasm   (f) Cell wall
   (b) Vacuole   (g) Chromosome
   (c) Starch granule   (h) Nuclear membrane
   (d) Chloroplast   (i) Endoplasmic reticulum
   (e) Mitochondria   (j) Plasma membrane

2. 9 cells (1 complete cell, plus the edges of 8 others)

3. Plant cell; it has chloroplasts and a cell wall. It also has a highly geometric cell shape.

4. (a) Cytoplasm located between the plasma membrane and nuclear membrane (extranuclear).
   (b) Composition of cytoplasm: A watery soup of dissolved substances. In eukaryotic cells, organelles are found in the cytoplasm. Cytoplasm = cytosol (including cytoskeleton) + organelles.
   (c) Prokaryotic cells do not have a defined nucleus.

5. (a) Starch granules, which occur within specialised plastids called leucoplasts. Starch granules are non-living inclusions, deposited as a reserve energy store.
   (b) Vacuoles, which are fluid filled cavities bounded by a single membrane. Plant vacuoles contain cell sap; an aqueous solution of dissolved food material, ions, waste products, and pigments. **Note**: Young plant cells (such as the one pictured) usually have several small vacuoles, which unite in a mature cell to form a large, permanent central vacuole.

Interpreting Electron Micrographs (page 80)

1. (a) Lysosome
   (b) Animal cells (the equivalent functions in plant cells and yeast is performed by lytic vacuoles).
   (c) Contains hydrolytic enzymes to digest excess or

worn-out organelles, food particles, and engulfed viruses or bacteria.

2. (a) Golgi apparatus
   (b) Plant and animal cells
   (c) Function: Packages substances to be secreted by the cell. Forms a membrane vesicle containing the chemicals for export from the cell (e.g. nerve cells export neurotransmitters; endocrine glands export hormones; digestive gland cells export enzymes).

3. (a) Mitochondrion
   (b) Plant and animal cells (most common in cells that have high energy demands, such as muscle).
   (c) Function: Site of most of the process of cellular respiration, which releases energy from food (glucose) to fuel metabolism.

(d)

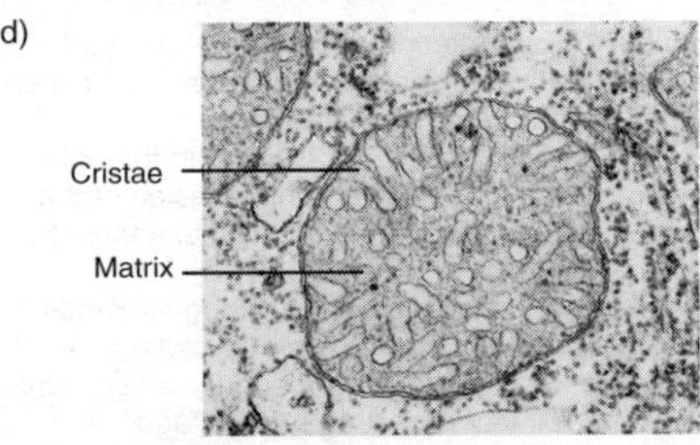

4. (a) Endoplasmic reticulum
   (b) Plant and animal cells (eukaryotes)
   (c) Function: Site of protein synthesis (translation stage). Transport network that moves substances through its system of tubes. Many complex reactions need to take place on the surface of the membranes.
   (d) Ribosomes.

5. (a) Nucleus
   (b) Plant and animal cells (eukaryotes)
   (c) Function: Controls cell metabolism (all the life-giving chemical reactions), and functioning of the whole organism. These instructions are inherited from one generation to the next.

(d)

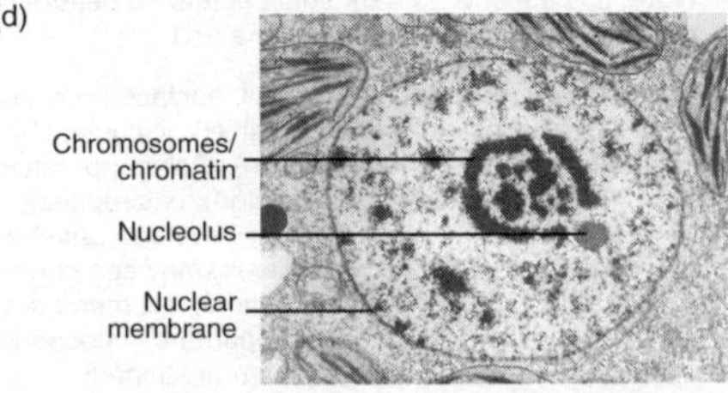

How Do We Know? Membrane Structure
(page 81)

1. Fixing a sample and then freezing it preserves its structure and allows it to be cleaved. The cleavage (splitting) process reveals internal structure. The techniques used in freeze fracture (splitting a lipid bilayer) and electron microscopy (coating in metals) reveal how proteins are organised in the membrane.

2. The impressions left in one side of the membrane after freeze fracture give evidence of proteins located within the membrane. Fracturing the membrane allowed scientists to observe the presence of integral membrane proteins which span the membrane lipid bilayer. This supported the fluid mosaic model, in which membrane bound proteins are able to move relatively freely within the membrane.

3. If the bilayer had a continuous protein coat, the freeze fracture specimen would look flat and uniform when viewed under the electron microscope.
The proteins are discrete complexes randomly spaced throughout the lipid bilayer. The bumps observed are where the proteins were located.

KEY TERMS: Crossword (page 82)

Answers Across

4. Mitochondria
7. Nucleolus
8. Cell wall
10. Ribosomes
12. Scanning electron microscopy
14. Golgi apparatus
16. Prokaryote
17. Plasma membrane
18. Flagella
19. Nucleus
20. Cytoplasm

Answers Down

1. Optical microscope
2. Endoplasmic reticulum
3. Eukaryote
5. Electron microscope
6. Capsule
9. Lysosomes
11. Cytoskeleton
13. Organelle
15. Stain

Cell Processes (page 84)

1. (a) Golgi apparatus
   (b) Cytoplasm, mitochondria
   (c) Plasma membrane, vacuoles
   (d) Plasma membrane, vacuoles
   (e) Endoplasmic reticulum, ribosomes, nucleus
   (f) Chloroplasts
   (g) Centrioles, nucleus
   (h) Lysosomes
   (i) Plasma membrane, Golgi apparatus

2. **Metabolism** describes all the chemical processes of life taking place inside the cell. Examples include cellular respiration, fatty acid oxidation, photosynthesis, digestion, urea cycle, and protein synthesis.

Lipids (page 85)

1. (a) Saturated fatty acids contain the maximum number of hydrogen atoms, whereas unsaturated fatty acids contain some double-bonded carbon atoms.
   (b) Saturated fatty acids tend to produce lipids that are solid at room temperature, whereas lipids that contain a high proportion of unsaturated fatty acids tend to be liquid at room temperature.

2. (a) Energy: Fats provide a compact, easily stored source of energy. Energy yield per gram on oxidation is twice that of carbohydrate.
   (b) Water: Metabolism of lipids releases water. **Note:** oxidation of triglycerides releases twice as much water as carbohydrate.
   (c) Insulation: Heat does not dissipate easily through fat therefore thick fat insulates against heat loss.

3. In **phospholipids**, one of the fatty acids is replaced with a phosphate; the molecule is ionised and the phosphate end is water soluble. **Triglycerides** are non-polar and not soluble in water.

4. Saturated fats are solid at room temperature because they comprise mostly saturated fatty acids. These contain the maximum number of hydrogen atoms and form straight molecules that pack tightly together.

5. (a) The amphipathic nature of phospholipids (with a polar, hydrophilic end and a hydrophobic, fatty acid end) causes them to orientate in aqueous solutions so that the hydrophobic 'tails' point in together. Hence the bilayer nature of phospholipid membranes.
   (c) The cellular membranes of an Arctic fish could be expected to contain a higher proportion of unsaturated fatty acids and more cholesterol than those of a tropical fish species. This would help them to remain fluid and functioning at low temperatures.

6. Cholesterol is an amphipathic molecule. It contains a hydroxyl (-OH) group as well a steroid ring structure and a hydrocarbon chain. The -OH group can interact with the polar head groups of the membrane phospholipids, stabilising the outer surface of the membrane and making it less permeable to some ions (less leaky). The steroid ring and hydrocarbon chain tuck into the hydrophobic part of the membrane, where the kinked structure increases membrane fluidity (in the same way that unsaturated fatty acids do) by preventing the phospholipids from packing too closely together.

The Structure of Membranes (page 87)

1. (a) Channel proteins and some carrier proteins.
   (b) Carrier proteins (ion pumps)
   (c) Glycoproteins and glycolipids
   (d) Cholesterol

2. (a) Membranes are composed of a phospholipid bilayer in which are embedded proteins, glycoproteins, and glycolipids. The structure is relatively fluid and the proteins are able to move within this fluid matrix.
   (b) This model accounts for the properties we observe in cellular membranes: its **fluidity** (how its shape is not static and how its components move within the membrane, relative to one-another) and its **mosaic nature** (the way in which the relative proportions of the membrane components, i.e. proteins, glycoproteins, glycolipids etc, can vary from membrane to membrane). The fluid mosaic model also accounts for how membranes can allow for the selective passage of materials (through protein channels for example) and how they enable cell-cell recognition (again, as a result of membrane components such as glycoproteins).

3. Membranes perform many diverse roles. The plasma membrane forms the outer limit of the cell and contains the proteins that confer cellular recognition. It also controls the entry and exit of materials into and out of the cell. Intracellular membranes keep the cytoplasm separate from the extracellular spaces and provide compartments within cells for localisation of metabolic (enzymatic) reactions. They also provide a surface for the attachment of the enzymes involved in metabolism.

4. (a) Any of: Golgi, mitochondria, chloroplasts, nucleus, endoplasmic reticulum, vacuoles, lysosomes.
    (b) Depends on choice: Generally the membrane's purpose is to compartmentalise the location of enzymatic reactions, to control the entry and exit of substances that the organelle operates on, and/or to provide a surface for enzyme attachment.

5. (a) Cholesterol lies between the phospholipids and prevents close packing. It thus functions to keep membranes more fluid. The greater the amount of cholesterol in the membrane the greater its fluidity.
    (b) At temperatures close to freezing, high proportions of membrane cholesterol is important in keeping membranes fluid and functioning.

6. (a)-(c) in any order: Oxygen, food (glucose), minerals and trace elements, water.

7. (a) Carbon dioxide   (b) Nitrogenous wastes

8.

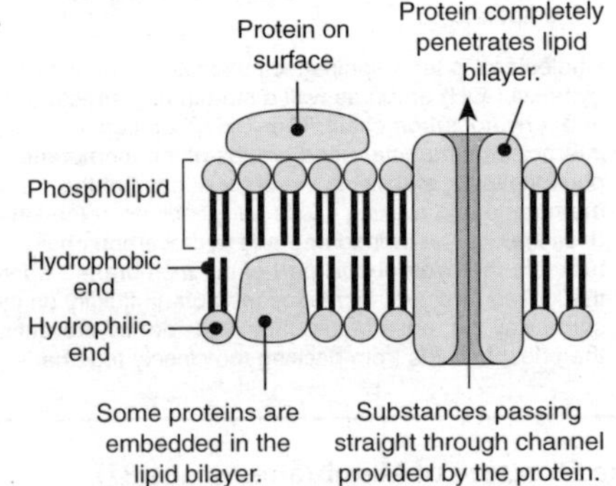

The Role of Membranes in Cells (page 89)

1. (a) Compartments within cells allow specific metabolic pathways in the cell to be localised. This achieves greater efficiency of cell function and restricts potentially harmful reactions and substances (e.g. hydrogen peroxide) to specific areas.
    (b) Greater membrane surface area provides a greater area over which membrane-bound reactions can occur. This increases the speed and efficiency with which metabolic reactions can take place.

2. (a) Golgi apparatus
    (b) lysosome
    (c) mitochondrion
    (d) rough endoplasmic reticulum
    (e) smooth endoplasmic reticulum
    (f) chloroplast

3. Membrane surface area is increased within cells and organelles by invaginations or by a long flattened shape which increases the surface area to volume ratio.

4. (a) High membrane surface area provides a greater area over which membrane-bound reactions can occur. This increases the speed and efficiency with which metabolic reactions can take place.
    (b) Channel and carrier proteins facilitate selective transport of substances through membranes. They can help to speed up the transport of substances into and out of the cell, especially for enzymatic reactions requiring a steady supply of substrate and constant removal of end-product, e.g. ADP supply to the mitochondrion during cellular respiration.

5. (a) Non-polar (lipid-soluble) molecules are able to dissolve in the lipid bilayer structure of the membrane and diffuse easily into the cell whereas the polar (lipid-insoluble) molecules have to be actively transported through the membrane.
    (b) Transportation of lipid-soluble molecules by diffusion alone into a cell is much quicker than that of lipid-insoluble molecules that have to be actively transported across the plasma membrane. This also increases the speed and efficiency with which metabolic reactions involving those molecules can take place.

Packaging Proteins (page 91)

1. (a) Rough ER: Ribosomes on the rough ER assemble the proteins destined for secretion.
    (b) Smooth ER: Synthesis of lipids, e.g. steroid hormones and phospholipids, and packages them into transport vesicles.
    (c) Golgi apparatus: Receives transport vesicles. Modifies, stores, and transports molecules for export around or from the cell.
    (d) Transport vesicles: These bud off the ER and move substances to the Golgi apparatus.

2. Polypeptides are synthesised by membrane bound ribosomes so that they can be easily threaded through the ER membrane into the cisternal space of the ER. Here they are in place for subsequent modification, packaging and export.

Passive Transport Processes (page 92)

1. (a) Large surface area
    (b) Thin membrane

2. (a) and (b) any of:
    – Molecules always move down a concentration gradient (from high to low concentration).
    – Molecules diffuse along their own concentration gradient, independent of other molecules (so two way diffusion is common in biological systems).
    – Diffusion rates are higher at higher temperatures.
    – Diffusion rates are faster when the concentration gradient is greater.
    – Thicker barriers slow diffusion.

3. (a) Channel-mediated facilitated diffusion, i.e through a protein channel in the membrane that creates a hydrophilic pore.
    (b) Carrier mediated facilitated diffusion, i.e. the molecule is aided across the membrane by a carrier protein specific to the molecule being transported.

4. Concentration gradients are maintained by (any one of): Constant use or transport away of a substance on one side of a membrane (e.g. use of ADP in mitochondria). Production of a substance on one side of a membrane (e.g. production of CO_2 by respiring cells).

5. Aquaporins are protein channels in the membrane specific to water molecules. This is faster (less resistance) than diffusion through the membrane.

6. (a) Zero
   (b) It water potential becomes more negative (lower)
   (c) Uptake of sucrose into the phloem (water follows passively by osmosis).

Ion Pumps (page 94)

1. ATP (directly or indirectly) supplies the energy to move substances against their concentration gradient.

2. (a) Cotransport describes coupling the movement of a molecule (such as sucrose or glucose) against its concentration gradient to the diffusion of an ion (e.g. H^+ or Na^+) down its concentration gradient. Note: An energy requiring ion exchange pump is used to establish this concentration gradient.
   (b) In the gut, a gradient in sodium ions is used to drive the transport of glucose across the epithelium. A Na^+/K^+ pump (requiring ATP) establishes an unequal concentration of Na^+ across the membrane. A specific membrane protein then couples the return of Na^+ down its concentration gradient to the transport of glucose (at a rate that is higher than could occur by diffusion alone).
   (c) The glucose diffuses from the epithelial cells of the gut into the blood, where it is transported away. This maintains a low level in the intestinal epithelial cells.

3. Extracellular accumulation of Na^+ (any two of):
   – maintains the gradient that is used to cotransport useful molecules, such as glucose, into cells.
   – maintains cell volume by creating an osmotic gradient that drives the absorption of water
   – establishes and maintains resting potential in nerve and muscle cells
   – provides the driving force for several facilitated membrane transport proteins

Exocytosis and Endocytosis (page 95)

1. **Phagocytosis** is the engulfment of solid material by endocytosis whereas **pinocytosis** is the uptake of liquids or fine suspensions by endocytosis.

2. Phagocytosis examples (any of):
   • Feeding in *Amoeba* by engulfment of material using cytoplasmic extensions called pseudopodia. • Ingestion of old red blood cells by Kupffer cells in the liver. • Ingestion of bacteria and cell debris by neutrophils and macrophages (phagocytic white blood cells).

3. Exocytosis examples (any of):
   • Secretion of substances from specialised secretory cells in multicellular organisms, e.g. hormones from endocrine cells, digestive secretions from exocrine cells. • Expulsion of wastes from unicellular organisms, e.g. *Paramecium* and *Amoeba* expelling residues from food vacuoles.

4. Any type of cytosis (unlike diffusion) is an active process involving the use of ATP. Low oxygen inhibits oxidative metabolism and lowers the energy yield from the respiration of substrates (ATP availability drops).

5. (a) **Oxygen**: Diffusion.
   (b) **Cellular debris**: Phagocytosis.
   (c) **Water**: Osmosis.
   (d) **Glucose**: Facilitated diffusion.

Active and Passive Transport Summary (page 69)

1. A. Diffusion
   B. Osmosis
   C. Facilitated diffusion
   D. Ion pump (or sodium-potassium pump)
   E. Pinocytosis
   F. Exocytosis
   E. Phagocytosis

2. **Passive transport** requires no energy input from the cell; materials follow a concentration gradient.
   Active transport requires considerable amounts of energy (ATP) to make materials go in a direction they would not normally go (at least at the rate required).

3. Gases moving by **diffusion**: Oxygen, carbon dioxide.

4. (a) Pinocytosis
   (b) Phagocytosis.
   (c) Osmosis
   (d) Exocytosis
   (e) Receptor-mediated endocytosis (see page 68)
   (f) Phagocytosis
   (g) Facilitated diffusion
   (h) Carrier-mediated facilitated diffusion (see page 64)
   (i) Sodium-potassium pump

Cholera (page 97)

1. The bacterium *Vibrio cholerae*.

2. If untreated, the copious diarrhoea can quickly lead to severe dehydration and a consequent collapse of all body systems (particularly kidney and heart failure).

3. Treatment with ORS provides replaces the electrolytes lost with the diarrhoea as well as the water. Glucose or sucrose in the ORS enhance electrolytes absorption. Drinking water alone does not address electrolyte loss.

4. When glucose is added to an ORS symptoms can worsen initially because the presence of sugars in the gut can make the diarrhoea worse (as a result of osmotic withdrawal of water into the gut lumen). This can cause people to stop treatment even though overall hydration is improved and electrolyte loss is reduced.

5. ORS deliver high concentrations of glucose and sodium ions to the gut lumen where they are transported into the epithelial cells by the sodium-glucose pump. Chloride ions follow the Na^+ into the cell, and then water follows down its osmotic gradient into the cell. Water can then enter the blood by osmosis to restore blood volume (the low blood volume caused by diarrhoeal dehydration lowers the water potential of the blood). **Teacher's note**: Glucose also leaves the epithelial cell and enters the bloodstream, but this is taken away and metabolised. Also note that the glucose transporter on the basal plasma membrane of the epithelial cell enables glucose to enter the interstitial space and then the blood by facilitated diffusion, unlike the glucose cotransporter which takes up glucose from the gut lumen into the cell.

6. Water and ion fluxes in response to cholera infection need to be understood to deliver an appropriate treatment. The first step is knowing that the cholera toxin affects chloride transport so that chloride ions enter the gut lumen at a higher rate than normal. Knowing that sodium ions and then water will follow

reveals the cause of the diarrhoea. A treatment that increases epithelial cell uptake of sodium and chloride to counteract these losses can then be devised.

7. The cholera toxin passes through the plasma membrane of the intestinal epithelial cell and acts as a signalling molecule, activating pathways that produce cyclic AMP from ATP. The cAMP opens the CFTR channels causing chloride ions to leave the cell and enter the gut lumen. Sodium ions follow the electrical gradient and water follows down its osmotic gradient, so salt (NaCl) and water leave the gut in copious amounts.

8. As with any trials, there is a risk that a new product may worsen the diarrhoea or have unexpected undesirable side effects. If a new product is ineffectual, there is a risk that the inadequacy of the treatment could be life threatening. The ethics of trials are especially fraught when the trials involve one group of patients receiving a placebo (no effect) or a less effective treatment (these are used to measure the extent to which the new product is better).

KEY TERMS: Word Find (page 99)

```
G G V Q I Z Y H N V I O N E X C H A N G E P U M P
C P H I E X O C Y T O S I S S G V X X G F U J L F
Q V X X G E H A M A A R O A U W I C B Q T N O E G
N E P A S S I V E T R A N S P O R T P J M A A W I
H N W D P G D A F E F E R W I G V T C T X L G X S
N D B F L U I D M O S A I C M O D E L V R I S H A
U O Q T A W W Z A C T I V E T R A N S P O R T Y X
G C Q Y Z T V S J B U R U E V P Z R P U O Q E C S
G Y E J W V U X R J H K B C I W O O E I H F X S D
R T R P H E Z X E Z M G D N E U T R A L F A T S C
B O F T Z K T I P H O S P H O L I P I D S G F H H
W S V D U C Q T G R C N B K A N A I Q X E S L L O
X I F F A V U K T M V D M S A T U R A T E D J X L
S S O H Y D R O L Y S I S I K K H F Z C R U L V E
Z K I I X N L X C C O N D E N S A T I O N L M D R
J Y D T T A Y O J V U H M H T W D G Y P X X B J A
F I M Q K L W Y P Z W F O T V Z C T O S M O S I S
W P T R I G L Y C E R I D E N L I P I D S B P C R
```

Introduction to Gas Exchange (page 101)

1. **Cellular respiration** refers to the production of ATP through the oxidation of glucose. **Gas exchange** refers to the way in which respiratory gases (oxygen and carbon dioxide) are exchanged with the environment. Oxygen is required to drive the reactions of cellular respiration. Carbon dioxide is a waste product.

2. (a) Moist so that gases can dissolve and diffuse across.
   (b) Large surface area to provide for a large amount of gas exchange (to meet the organism's needs).
   (c) Thin membrane that does not present a large barrier to diffusion of gases. This provides a surface across which gases easily diffuse.

3. The rate of diffusion across the gas exchange surface will be more rapid when membrane surface area or concentration difference across the membrane increases and/or membrane thickness decreases.

Breathing in Humans (page 102)

1. **Breathing** ventilates the lungs, renewing the supply of fresh (high oxygen) air while expelling high carbo dioxide air (CO_2 gained as a result of gas exchanges in the tissues).

2. (a) **Quiet breathing**: External intercostal muscles and diaphragm contract. Lung space increases and air flows into the lungs (inspiration). Inflation is detected and breath in ends. Expiration occurs through elastic recoil of the ribcage and lung tissue (air flows passively out to equalise with outside air pressure).
   (b) During forced or **active breathing**, muscular contraction is involved in both the inspiration and the expiration (expiration is not passive).

3. Water vapour

4. The elasticity of the lung tissue enable natural recoil of the lungs during quiet breathing so that expiration is a passive process not requiring energy.

5. Blood pH is a good indicator of high carbon dioxide levels, since increased CO_2 levels cause blood pH to fall. This indicates a need to increase respiratory rate to remove the CO_2 (and obtain more oxygen).

The Human Gas Exchange System (page 103)

1. (a) The structural arrangement (lobes, each with its own bronchus and dividing many times before terminating in numerous alveoli) provides an immense surface area for gas exchange.
   (b) Gas exchange takes place in the alveoli.

2. The respiratory membrane is the layered junction between the alveolar cells, the endothelial cells of the capillaries, and their associated basement membranes. It provides a surface across which gases can freely move.

3. Surfactant reduces the surface tension of the lung tissue and counteracts the tendency of the alveoli to recoil inward and stick together after each expiration.

4. Completed table as below:

	Region	Cartilage	Ciliated epithelium	Goblet cells (mucus)	Smooth muscle	Connective tissue
1	Trachea	✓	✓	✓	✓	✓
2	Bronchus	✓	✓	✓	✓	✓
3	Bronchioles	gradually lost	✓	✓	✓	✓
4	Alveolar duct	✗	✗	✗	✓	✓
5	Alveoli	✗	✗	✗	very little	✓

5. Respiratory distress syndrome: The lack of surfactant and high surface tension in the alveoli result in the collapse of the lungs to an uninflated state after each breath. Breathing is difficult and laboured, oxygen delivery is inadequate and, if untreated, death usually follows in a few hours.

Measuring Lung Function (page 105)

1. (a) Taller people generally have larger lung volumes and capacities.
   (b) Males have larger lung volumes and capacities than females.
   (c) After adulthood, lung volume and capacity declines with age. Children have smaller lung volumes and lung capacities than adults.

2. (a) Forced volume is a more useful indicator of impairment of lung function than a tidal volume because people use only a small proportion of their lung volume in normal breathing.
   (b) Spirometry can be used to measure the extent of recovery of lung function after treatment.

3. (a) Tidal volume   vol: $0.5 \ dm^3$
   (b) Expiratory reserve volume   vol: $1.0 \ dm^3$
   (c) Residual volume   vol: $1.2 \ dm^3$
   (d) Inspiratory capacity   vol: $3.8 \ dm^3$
   (e) Vital capacity   vol: $4.8 \ dm^3$
   (f) Total lung capacity   vol: $6.0 \ dm^3$

4. G: Tidal volume is increasing as a result of exercise.

5. PV: $15 \times 0.4 = 6 \ dm^3$

6. (a) During strenuous exercise, PV increases markedly.
   (b) Increased PV is achieved as a result of an increase in both breathing rate and tidal volume.

7. (a) There is 90X more CO_2 in exhaled air than in inhaled air ($3.6 \div 0.04$).
   (b) The CO_2 is the product of cellular respiration in the tissues. Note: Some texts give a value of 4.0% for exhaled air (100X the CO_2 content of inhaled air).
   (c) The dead space air is not involved in gas exchange therefore retains a higher oxygen content than the air that leaves the alveoli air. This raises the oxygen content of the expired air.

Gas Transport in Humans (page 107)

1. (a) Oxygen is high in the lung alveoli and in the capillaries leaving the lung.
   (b) Carbon dioxide is high in the capillaries leaving the tissues and in the cells of the body tissues.

2. Haemoglobin can bind oxygen reversibly, so it can take up oxygen when the oxygen pressures are high (lungs), and carry oxygen to where it is required (the tissues) and release it.

3. (a) Because CO binds so strongly, it quickly occupies all the binding sites of the haemoglobin molecules so that there is very little oxygen carried. The tissues become oxygen deprived and die.
   (b) The blood of smokers has CO in it (from cigarette smoke) and therefore has a much lower oxygen carrying capacity.

Review of Lung Function (page 108)

1. (a) Nasal cavity   (i)   Asthma
   (b) Oral cavity   (ii)   Emphysema
   (c) Trachea   (iii)   Pulmonary tuberculosis
   (d) Lung   (iv)   Fibrosis
   (e) Terminal bronchiole

    (f) Alveoli
    (g) Diaphragm

2. A = Inspiratory reserve volume   vol: $3.3 \ dm^3$
   B = Inspiratory capacity   vol: $3.8 \ dm^3$
   C = Tidal volume   vol: $0.5 \ dm^3$
   D = Expiratory reserve volume   vol: $1.0 \ dm^3$
   E = Residual volume   vol: $1.2 \ dm^3$

Respiratory Diseases (page 109)

1. Obstructive lung diseases are those in which the air cannot reach the gas exchange region of the lung, as occurs as a result of airway constriction (asthma), excess mucus (bronchitis), or reduced lung elasticity (emphysema). Restrictive lung diseases result from scarring of the gas exchange surface (fibrosis) which results in stiffening and lack of lung expansion. Such diseases result from inhalation of dusts (e.g. coal dust).

2. (a) In a chronic obstructive pulmonary disease, the FEV_1 is reduced disproportionately more than the FVC resulting in an FEV_1/FVC ratio less than 70%.
   (b) Although the FEV_1/FVC ratio is reduced in asthmatics, there will be an improvement in the ratio towards the normal range (80%+) after treatment.
   (c) In a restrictive lung disease, both FEV1 and the FVC are compromised equally, so even though measures of lung function indicate impairment the FEV1/FVC ratio remains high.

3. Restrictive lung diseases, such as **fibrosis**, impair lung function because the gas exchange surface becomes scarred, less flexible, and thicker. This reduces the amount of alveolar expansion possible and reduces the diffusion efficiency across the gas exchange surface.

4. Many restrictive diseases are caused by inhalation of dusts and pollutants associated with particular occupations, e.g. asbestos workers, coal miners, beryllium miners, cement workers etc.

5. In an asthma attack, histamine is released from sensitised mast cells. The histamine causes airway constriction, accumulation of fluid and mucus, and inability to breathe.

Smoking and the Lungs (page 111)

1. Long-term smoking results in increased production of mucus (in an attempt to trap and rid the lungs of smoke particles). This lung tissue is irritated and a cough develops associated with removing the excess mucus. The smoke particles indirectly destroy the alveolar walls, leading to coalescing of the alveoli and a substantial loss of lung surface area. The toxins in the smoke and tar damage the DNA of cells and lead to cancerous cells and tumours.

2. (a) **Tars**: Cause chronic irritation of the respiratory system and are also carcinogenic
   (b) **Nicotine**: Addictive component of tobacco smoke
   (c) **Carbon monoxide**: Markedly reduces the oxygen carrying capacity of the blood by binding to haemoglobin and forming a stable carboxy-haemoglobin compound. CO has a very high affinity for Hb (higher than that of oxygen) and will preferentially occupy oxygen binding sites. It is released only slowly for the body.

3. (a) **Emphysema**: Increasing shortness of breath (which becomes increasingly more severe until it is present even at rest). Chest becomes barrel shaped (associated with air being trapped in the outer part of the lungs). Often accompanied by a chronic cough and wheeze (caused by the distension (damage and coalescing) of the alveoli). **Note**: Chronic bronchitis and emphysema are often together called chronic obstructive lung disease.

   (b) **Chronic bronchitis**: A condition in which sputum (phlegm) is coughed up on most days during at least three consecutive months in at least two consecutive years. The disease results in widespread narrowing and obstruction of the airways in the lungs and often occurs with or contributes to emphysema.

   (c) **Lung cancer**: Impaired lung function; coughing up blood, chest pain, breathlessness, and death.

4. (a) A long term study is important with a chronic disease that develops slowly because it may take many years for convincing relationships to become evident in the data.

   (b) The study also showed that there was a convincing 20 year lag in the development of lung cancer in smokers.

Living with Chronic Lung Disease (page 113)

1. The economic impact of tobacco smoking-related diseases is two fold. Directly there are the considerable heath costs associated with treating the consequences of diseases such as chronic bronchitis and emphysema, which often require repeated and prolonged hospital visits. Secondly, there is the economic cost of lost work days (estimated 24 million lost work days per annum).

2. This response is largely a student's own and there is no 'right' answer. Tobacco-related diseases generally have a detrimental effect on a person's quality of life and on the quality of life for those who end up as carers for debilitated relatives. There are additional associated health costs with hospital and doctor's visits and treatments, and the stress of living with a chronic condition which leaves the sufferer vulnerable to more serious lung infections. Personal testimonials, such as that from Jenny's daughter, provide a first hand account of what the personal costs can be and may give some people enough reason to reconsider their smoking habit or to stop them ever taking it up.

Tuberculosis (page 114)

1. (a) Inhalation of the TB pathogen results in a defence response from the lung macrophages, leading to formation of tubercles (nodules) in the lung tissue which can rupture through the alveolar walls to release infective bacteria into the airways. These regions are replaced by scarring and areas of necrotic (dying) tissue which are ineffective for gas exchange. Fluid accumulation is associated with this. The greater the extent of infection, the more congestion, scarring and necrosis, and the greater the amount of gas exchange surface lost.

   (b) TB is transmitted by airborne droplets, which are coughed or sneezed out following the rupture of tubercles, which releases bacilli into the airways.

2. The body's immune response is capable of walling-off the bacteria in nodules (tubercles). In this dormant state, the bacteria do not have the capacity to cause disease symptoms and the person is not infectious.

KEY TERMS: Mix and Match (page 115)

Alveoli (V), Breathing (Y), Breathing rate (S), Bronchi (U), Bronchioles (M), Carbon dioxide (N), Cartilage (P), Cellular respiration (Z), Diaphragm (A), Emphysema (AA), Expiration (B), Fick's law (F), Gas exchange surface (E), Gas exchange system (Q), Goblet cells (C), Inspiration (W), Intercostal muscles (I), Lungs (T), Oxygen (G), Pulmonary tuberculosis (L), Pulmonary ventilation rate (X), Spirometry (H), Surfactant (D), Tidal volume (O), Trachea (R), Ventilation (J), Vital capacity (K)

The Human Heart (page 117)

1. (a) Pulmonary artery   (e) Aorta
   (b) Vena cava   (f) Pulmonary vein
   (c) Right atrium   (g) Left atrium
   (d) Right ventricle   (h) Left ventricle

Positions of heart valves

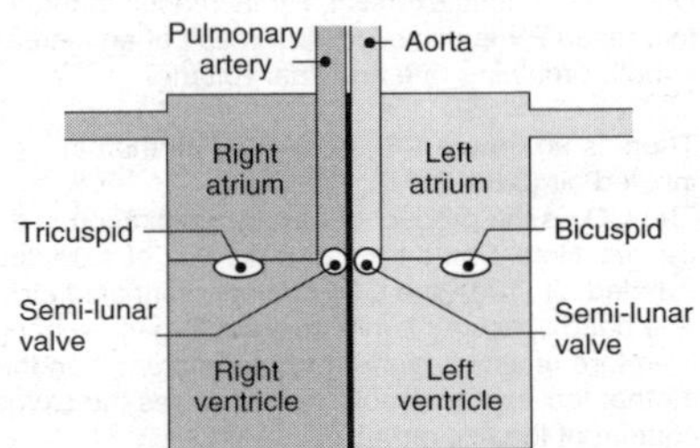

2. **Valves** prevent the blood from flowing the wrong way through the heart and help regulate filling of the chambers.

3. (a) The heart has its own coronary blood supply to meet the high oxygen demands of the heart tissue.

   (b) There must be a system within the heart muscle itself to return deoxygenated blood and waste products of metabolism back to the right atrium.

4. If blood flow to a particular part of the heart is restricted or blocked (because of blocked blood vessel), the part of the heart muscle supplied by that vessel will die, leading to a heart attack or infarction.

5. A: arterioles   B: venules
   C: arterioles   D: capillaries

6. (a) The **pulse pressure** is the difference between the systolic pressure and the diastolic pressure.

   (b) Pulse pressure between the aorta and the capillaries will decrease (because of the increasing resistance met on route).

7. (a) You are recording expansion and recoil of the artery that occurs with each contraction of the left ventricle.

   (b) The best place to take a **pulse** is from the brachial or carotid artery. The blood flow from these arteries (close to the heart) is at a high pressure and still carries the beat or pulse.

The Cardiac Cycle (page 123)

1. (a) QRS complex   (b) T   (c) P

2. During the period of electrical recovery the heart muscle cannot contract. This ensures that the heart has an enforced rest and will not fatigue, nor accumulate lactic acid (as occurs in working skeletal muscle).

3. Extra text removed and letter answers have been placed for each cycle.

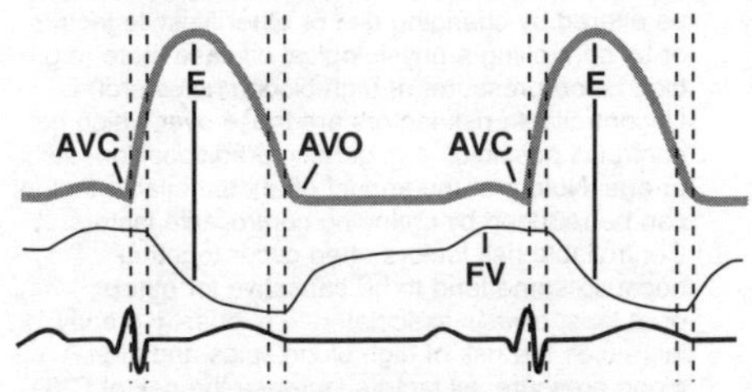

Control of Heart Activity (page 120)

1. (a) **Sinoatrial node**: Initiates the cardiac cycle through the spontaneous generation of action potentials.
   (b) **Atrioventricular node**: Delays the impulse.
   (c) **Bundle of His**: Distributes the action potentials over the ventricles (resulting in ventricular contraction).
   (d) **Intercalated discs**: Electrical junctions that allow the action potentials to spread rapidly through the heart muscle.

2. (a) The heart muscle is capable of rhythmic contraction independently of any external nervous stimulation.
   (b) When the heart is removed from its nervous supply (if provided with adequate oxygen, ions, and fluids) will continue to beat.

3. Delaying the impulse at the AVN allows time for atrial contraction to finish before the ventricles contract.

Exercise and Blood Flow (page 121)

1. Answers for missing values are listed from top to bottom under the appropriate heading:

	At rest (% of total)	Exercise (% of total)
Heart	4.0	4.2
Lung	2.0	1.1
Kidneys	22.0	3.4
Liver	27.0	3.4
Muscle	15.0	70.2
Bone	5.0	1.4
Skin	6.0	10.7
Thyroid	1.0	0.3
Adrenals	0.5	0.1
Other	3.5	1.0

2. The heart beats faster and harder to increase the volume of blood pumped per beat and the number of beats per minute (increased blood flow).

3. (a) Blood flow increases approximately 3.5 times.
   (b) Working tissues require more oxygen and nutrients than can be delivered by a resting rate of blood flow. Therefore the rate of blood flow (delivery to the tissues) must increase during exercise.

4. (a) Thyroid and adrenal glands, as well as the tissues other than those defined in the table, show no change in absolute rate of blood flow.
   (b) This is because they are not involved in exercise and do not require an increased blood flow. However, they do need to maintain their usual blood supply and cannot tolerate an absolute decline.

5. (a) Skeletal muscles (increases 16.7X), skin (increases 6.3X), and heart (increases 3.7X)
   (b) These tissues and organs are all directly involved in the exercise process and need a greater rate of supply of oxygen and nutrients. Skeletal muscles move the body, the heart must pump a greater volume of blood at a greater rate and the skin must help cool the body to maintain core temperature.

6. Heart size increases because (like any muscle) it gets bigger with work. The larger size also means it pumps a greater volume of blood more efficiently.

7. Endurance athletes have a smaller body weight.

8. With each stroke, the heart pumps a larger volume of blood. Less energy is expended in pumping the same volume of blood.

9. A lower resting heart rate means that for most of the time, the heart is not working as hard as in someone with a higher resting heart rate.

The Health Benefits of Exercise (page 123)

1. (a) Blood flow rate is increased during exercise through increased rate and force of heart contraction and skeletal muscle contraction, and dilation of blood vessels.
   (b) Physiological effects of regular exercise include: An increase in muscular strength and flexibility, more efficient heart function, improvement in immune function, increased concentration, and higher energy levels.
   (c) These changes in physiology equip the body to handle the usual, everyday events of life with less effort and stress. Ongoing benefits include improved blood flow and more efficient organ function, faster tissue repair, better weight control, improved sleep and stress management, and better immune function. **Note**: These benefits do not extend to over-training, when stresses exceed the health benefits gained from exercise.

2. (a) **Increase in stroke volume and cardiac output**:
   Health benefits: Lower resting heart rate, lower blood pressure and improved cardiovascular performance.
   Physiological mechanism: Increases the volume of blood transported with each beat to and from the working tissues.
   (b) **Increased ventilation efficiency**:
   Health benefits: Regular breathing is easier to sustain with less effort required during periods of activity. Physiological mechanism: Increases the rate of gas exchange (oxygen transported into and

carbon dioxide transported out of the blood).

(c) **Increase in lean muscle and decreased body fat**:
<u>Health benefits</u>: General increase in level of fitness and muscular performance with the various physiological and psychological benefits that stem from this.
<u>Physiological mechanism</u>: An increase in the amount of muscle tissue that can be recruited into work and a decrease in the amount of non-active tissue (fat) that must be moved around.

(d) **Increased muscular strength and endurance**:
<u>Health benefits</u>: Improved stamina and less chance of injury when exercising.
<u>Physiological mechanism</u>: Improvements in cardiovascular and ventilation performance and greater resilience during activity.

(e) **Maintenance of stable, healthy body weight**:
<u>Health benefits</u>: Decline in the risk of suffering heart disease and other associated illnesses.
<u>Physiological mechanism</u>: Controls weight by reducing body fat and building muscle and improves the metabolism of food by the body.

3. Irregular or very low intensity exercise does not improve the body's cardiovascular performance or ventilation efficiency because the body is not challenged frequently enough to adapt to the stress of repeated exercise. In fact, irregular exercise may contribute to physiological stress in an unfit individual.

Cardiovascular Disease (page 125)

1. Cardiovascular disease (CVD) refers to a class of diseases that affect the cardiovascular system (the heart or the blood vessels).

2. **Congenital CVD** refers to cardiovascular problems that a person is born with. They can be inherited, the result of viral infections, or the result of genetic defects (mutations). In contrast, **acquired CVD** describes cardiovascular diseases arising during the course of a person's life. They are mostly the result of environmental or lifestyle factors, but can sometimes be the result of genetics.

3. CVD is a major public health concern because it is so widespread, accounting for 34% of deaths in the UK and billions of pounds in lost productivity and heath care costs. Importantly, many of the risk factors associated with CVD are preventable, so education and public health management has a role to play in reducing the levels of CVD in the population.

Atherosclerosis (page 126)

1. Even though a plaque is forming, blood can continue to flow relatively unhindered through blood vessels. It is only when the blood vessel is almost completely obstructed that symptoms arise. Fit, healthy people may not show any symptoms at all until a plaque ruptures and causes a major blood clot, which can be lethal.

2. Atherosclerosis is triggered when a vessel is damaged (e.g. by oxidised LDLs or persistent hypertension). LDLs accumulate at the damaged site and macrophages follow forming foam cells. The foam cells accumulate to form an intermediate lesion called a plaque. As the atheroma develops, the smooth muscle cells of the

blood vessel die, and scar tissue forms. Calcium salts accumulate forming and complicated plaque and the arterial wall may ulcerate. The plaque may break away forming a clot, which may be fatal.

3. People with atherosclerosis are more at risk of suffering an aneurysm, stroke, or heart attack. This is because their blood vessels may become blocked from the plaque or by a blood clot resulting from an atherosclerotic plaque which has broken off and entered the circulation.

Risk Factors for CVD (page 127)

1. (a) Controllable risk factors for CVD are those that can be altered by changing diet or other lifestyle factors, or by controlling a physiological disease state (e.g. high blood pressure, or high blood cholesterol). Uncontrollable risk factors are those over which no control is possible, e.g. genetic predisposition, sex, or age. Note that the impact of uncontrollable factors can be reduced by changing controllable factors.

   (b) Controllable risk factors often occur together because some tend to be causative for others, or at least always associated, e.g. obesity greatly increases the risk of high blood lipids and high blood pressure: all factors increase the risk of CVD.

   (c) Those with several risk factors have a higher chance of developing CVD because the risks are cumulative and add up to pose a greater total risk.

2. (a) LDL deposits cholesterol on the endothelial lining of blood vessels, whereas HDL transports cholesterol to the liver where it is processed. A high LDL:HDL ratio is more likely to result in CVD because more cholesterol will be deposited on blood vessels and contribute to atherosclerosis.

   (b) The LDL:HDL ratio is a more accurate predictor of heart disease risk than total cholesterol *per se*, since it more accurately indicates how much cholesterol will be deposited in arteries.

3. (a) Obesity operates as a risk factor by creating a greater work load for the heart (blood must be pumped through a greater mass of tissue) and exacerbating hypertension. The evidence for this link is quite clear in both men and women; the percentage of men and women developing coronary heart disease is much higher in the obese (BMI 30 and above) than in people of normal weight.

   (b) CHD risk increases again in people of low BMI because of inadequate nutrition (nearing starvation levels), which often results in electrolyte imbalances and consequently heart strain and arryhthmia.

Reducing the Risk (page 129)

1. Deaths from CHD have steadily fallen since 1970. Current levels are approximately 60% less than in 1970.

   (b) Rates of smoking in adults have steadily declined over time. They are approximately half the level they were in 1970.

2. (a) There is a strong correlation between CHD deaths and smoking rates; they have been declining together since the 1970s.

   (b) No; a correlation, even a strong one, does not prove direct causation. However, the link can be made on the weight of other supporting evidence.

3. Public health education programmes present information gathered from scientific studies in a simple and easily understood way. They can help raise awareness in the public, and potentially bring about widespread change. The effectiveness of these campaigns varies; a successful campaign can take a lot of time and money, but can have the potential to save millions in health care and related expenses.

Review of the Human Heart (page 130)

1. (1)   Anterior vena cava
   (2)   Right atrium
   (3)   Sinoatrial node (SAN)
   (4)   Atrioventricular node (AVN)
   (5) Bundle of His (atrioventricular bundle)
   (6)   Right ventricle
   (7)   Left common carotid
   (8)   Left subclavian artery
   (9)   Aorta
   (10) Pulmonary artery
   (11) Left atrium
   (12) Purkyne fibres
   (13) Left ventricle

2. A =   Contraction of the atria.
   B =   Contraction of the ventricles.
   C =   Relaxation and recovery of ventricles.

3. 70 cm^3 X 70 beats per min. = 4900 cm^3 = 4.9 dm^3.

KEY TERMS: Crossword (page 131)

Answers Across

1. Cardiac output
3. Diastole
8. Purkyne tissue
10. Cardiac cycle
11. Semilunar valves
12. Sinoatrial node
16. Coronary arteries
17. Myocardial infarction
18. Atrioventricular node
19. Atherosclerosis

Answers Down

2. Intrinsic heart rate
4. Aorta
5. Pulmonary artery
6. Hypertension
7. Ventricle
9. Electrocardiogram
13. Systole
14. Stroke volume
15. Atrium

The First Line of Defence (page 133)

1. The natural population of (normally non-pathogenic) microbes can benefit the host by preventing overgrowth of pathogens (through competitive exclusion).

2. The skin provides a physical barrier to prevent pathogens entering the body. Skin secretions (serum and sweat) contain antimicrobial chemicals that inhibit microbial growth.

3. (a) **Phospholipases** kill bacteria by hydrolysing the phospholipids in cell walls and membranes.
   (b) **Cilia** moves the microbes, which are trapped in mucus towards the mouth and nostrils., where they can be expelled.
   (c) Sebum has antimicrobial activity and (with sweat) a pH that is unfavourable for microbial growth.

The Body's Defences (page 134)

1. **Specific resistance** refers to defence against particular (identified) pathogens. It involves a range of specific responses to the pathogen concerned (antibody production and cell-mediated immunity). In contrast, **non-specific resistance** refers to defence against any type of pathogen. it takes the form of physical and chemical barriers against infection, as well as phagocytosis and inflammation.

2. (a) **Phagocytosis** destroys pathogens directly by engulfing them.
   (b) Antimicrobial substances (e.g. **interferon**) prevent multiplication of microbes (especially viruses).
   (c) Antibodies are produced against specific pathogens, and bind and destroy pathogens or their toxins.

3. A hierarchical system of defence provides a series of back-ups in case a pathogen breaches earlier barriers. Most microbes are excluded by the first line of defence, but those that penetrate the skin will usually be destroyed by white blood cells and the chemicals associated with inflammation. Failing this, the body will mount a targeted specific defence against the identified pathogen still remaining.

The Action of Phagocytes (page 135)

1. Neutrophils, eosinophils, macrophages.

2. By looking at the ratio of white blood cells to red blood cells (not involved in the immune response). An elevated white blood cell count (specifically a high neutrophil count) indicates microbial infection.

3. Microbes may be able to produce toxins that kill phagocytes directly. Others can enter the phagocytes, completely filling them and preventing them functioning or remaining dormant and resuming activity later.

Inflammation (page 136)

1. (a) **Increased diameter and permeability of blood vessels**. Purpose: Increases blood flow and delivery of leucocytes to the area. Aids removal of destroyed microbes or their toxins. Allows defensive substances to leak into the tissue spaces.
   (b) **Phagocyte migration and phagocytosis**. Purpose: To directly attack and destroy invading microbes and foreign substances.
   (c) **Tissue repair**. Purpose: Replaces damaged cells and tissues, restoring the integrity of the area.

2. Phagocytic features: Ability to squeeze through capillary walls (amoeboid movement), and ability to engulf material by phagocytosis.

3. Histamines and prostaglandins attract phagocytes to the site of infection.

4. **Pus** is the accumulated debris of infection (dead phagocytes, damaged tissue, and fluid). It accumulates at the site of infection where the defence process is most active.

Fever (page 137)

1. The high body temperature associated with fever intensifies the action of interferon (a potent antiviral substance). Fever also increases metabolism, which is associated with increased blood flow. These changes increase the rate at which white blood cells are delivered to the site of infection and help to speed up the repair of tissues. The release of interleukin-1 during fever helps to increase the production of T cell lymphocytes and speeds up the immune response.

2. **1:** Macrophage ingests a microbe and destroys it.
   2: The release of endotoxins from the microbe induces the macrophage to produce interleukin-1 which is released into the blood.
   3: Interleukin-1 travels in the blood to the hypothalamus of the brain where it stimulates the production of large amounts of prostaglandins.
   4: Prostaglandins cause resetting of the thermostat to a higher temperature, causing fever.

Blood Clotting and Defence (page 138)

1. (a) Prevents bleeding and invasion of bacteria.
   (b) Aids in the maintenance of blood volume.

2. (a) Injury exposes collagen fibres to the blood.
   (b) Chemicals make the surrounding platelets sticky.
   (c) Clumping forms an immediate plug of platelets preventing blood loss.
   (d) Fibrin clot traps red blood cells and reinforces the seal against blood loss.

3. (a) Clotting factors catalyse the conversion of prothrombin to thrombin, the active enzyme that catalyses the production of fibrin.
   (b) If the clotting factors were present all the time, the clotting could not be contained and the blood would clot when it should not.

4. (a) and (b) provided below. The first is the obvious answer, but there are disorders associated with the absence of each of the twelve clotting factors:
   (a) Classic haemophilia.
   (b) Clotting factor VIII (anti-haemophiliac factor).

   (a) Haemophilia B (Christmas disease).
   (b) Clotting factor IX (Christmas factor).

Blood (page 139)

1. **Note**: In some cases, the answers below provide more detail than expected. This is provided as extension.
   (b) Protection against disease:
   Blood component: White blood cells
   Mode of action: Engulf bacteria, mediate immune reactions, and allergic and inflammatory responses.
   (c) Communication between cells, tissues and organs:
   Blood component: Hormones
   Mode of action: Specific chemicals which are carried in the blood to target tissues, where they interact with specific receptors and bring about an appropriate response.
   (d) Oxygen transport:
   Blood component: Haemoglobin molecule of erythrocytes.
   Mode of action: Binds oxygen at the lungs and releases it at the tissues.
   (e) Carbon dioxide transport:
   Blood components: Mainly plasma (most carbon dioxide is carried as bicarbonate in the plasma, a small amount is dissolved in the plasma). Red blood cells (a small amount (10-20%) of carbon dioxide is carried bound to haemoglobin).
   Mode of action: Diffuses between tissues, plasma, and lungs according to concentration gradient.
   (f) Buffer against pH changes:
   Blood components: Haemoglobin molecule of erythrocytes. Plasma bicarbonate and proteins.
   Mode of action: Free hydrogen ions are picked up and carried by the haemoglobin molecule (removed from solution). Plasma bicarbonate can form either carbonic acid by picking up a hydrogen ion (H^+), or sodium bicarbonate by combining with sodium ions. Negatively charged proteins also associate with H^+.
   (g) Nutrient supply:
   Blood component: Plasma
   Mode of action: Glucose is carried in the plasma and is taken up by cells (made available throughout the body to all tissues).
   (h) Tissue repair:
   Blood components: Platelets and leucocytes
   Mode of action: Platelets initiate the cascade of reactions involved in clotting and wound repair. Leucocytes (some types) engulf bacteria and foreign material, preventing or halting infection.
   (i) Transport of hormones, lipids, and fat soluble vitamins:
   Blood component: α-globulins
   Mode of action: α-globulins bind these substances and carry them in the plasma. This prevents them being filtered in the kidneys and lost in the urine.

2. Any of: Presence (WBC) or absence (RBC) of **nucleus**. Colour, reflecting presence (RBC) or absence (WBC) of respiratory pigment, **haemoglobin**. **Shape and size** (smaller, dish shaped RBCs vs larger, rounded WBCs. **Mitochondria** present in WBCs, absent in RBCs.

3. (a) Lack of a nucleus allows more space inside the cell to carry Hb (hence greater O_2 carrying capacity).
   (b) Lack of mitochondria forces the red blood cells to metabolise anaerobically so that they do not consume the oxygen they are carrying.

4. (a) Elevated eosinophil count: Allergic response such as hay fever or asthma.
   (b) Elevated neutrophil count: Microbial infection.
   (c) Elevated basophil count: Inflammatory response e.g. as a result of an allergy or a parasitic (as opposed to bacterial) infection.
   (d) Elevated lymphocyte count: Infection or response to vaccination.

Acquired Immunity (page 141)

1. (a) **Passive immunity** describes the immunity that develops after antibodies are transferred from one person to another. In this case, the recipient does not make the antibodies themselves.
   (b) **Naturally acquired** passive immunity arises as a result of antibodies passing from the mother to the foetus/infant via the placenta/breast milk. **Artificially acquired** passive immunity arises as a result of injection with immune serums e.g. in antivenoms.

2. (a) Newborns need to be supplied with maternal antibodies because they have not yet had exposure

to the everyday microbes in their environment and must be born with operational defence mechanisms.

(b) The antibody "supply" is (ideally) supplemented with antibodies in breast milk because it takes time for the infant's immune system to become fully functional. During this time, the supply of antibodies received during pregnancy will decline.

(c) Breast feeding will provide the infant with a naturally acquired passive immunity to help protect it against infections while its immune system develops. Without this acquisition, your infant is more likely to be vulnerable to everyday infections against which you already have immunity but he/she does not.

3. (a) **Active immunity** is immunity that develops after the body has been exposed to a microbe or its toxins and an immune response has been invoked.

(b) **Naturally acquired** active immunity arises as a result of exposure to an antigen such as a pathogen, e.g. natural immunity to chickenpox. **Artificially acquired** active immunity arises as a result of vaccination, e.g. any childhood disease for which vaccinations are given: diphtheria, measles, mumps, polio etc.

4. (a) The primary response is less pronounced (smaller magnitude) than the secondary response. The primary response takes longer to develop and is over more quickly than the secondary response, which is rapid and long lasting.

(b) The immune system has already been "primed" or prepared to respond to the antigen by the first exposure to it. When the cells of the immune system receive a second exposure to the same antigen they can respond quickly with rapid production of antibodies.

5. (a) Herd immunity refers to the protection that unimmunised people have against a circulating disease by virtue of the fact that most of the population are immunised.

(b) A fall in vaccination rates is a concern because, once the population contains a high proportion of non-vaccinated people, herd immunity is lost and a circulating disease can spread very rapidly through the community, raising public health costs and contributing to lost productivity.

The Immune System (page 143)

1. (a) **Humoral immune system**: Production of antibodies against specific antigens. The antibodies disable circulating antigens.

(b) **Cell-mediated immune system**: Involves the production of T cells which destroy pathogens or their toxins by direct contact or by producing substances that regulate the activity of other cells in the immune system.

2. In the bone marrow (adults) or liver (foetuses).

3. (a) Bone marrow   (b) Thymus

4. (a) **Memory cells**: Retain an antigen memory. They can rapidly differentiate into antibody- producing plasma cells if they encounter the same antigen again.

(b) **Plasma cells**: Secrete antibodies against antigens (very rapid rate of antibody production).

(c) **Helper T cells**: Activate cytotoxic T cells and other helper T cells. Also needed for B cell activation.

(d) **Suppressor T cells**: Regulate the immune system response by turning it off when antigens disappear.

(e) **Delayed hypersensitivity T cells**: Cause inflammation in allergic responses and are responsible for rejection of transplanted tissue.

(f) **Cytotoxic T cells**: Destroy target cells on contact (by binding and lysing cells).

5. **Immunological memory**: The result of the differentiation of B cells after the first exposure to an antigen. Those B cells that differentiate into long lived memory cells are present to react quickly and vigorously in the event of a second infection.

Antibodies (page 145)

1. **Antibodies** are proteins produced in response to antigens; they recognise and bind antigens. **Antigens** are foreign substances (often proteins) that promote the formation of antibodies (invoke an immune response).

2. (a) The immune system must be able to recognise self from non-self so that it can recognise foreign material (and destroy it) and its own tissue (and not destroy it).

(b) During development, any B cells that react to the body's own antigens are selectively destroyed. This process leads to self tolerance.

(c) Autoimmune disease (disorder).

(d) Any two of: Grave's disease (thyroid enlargement), rheumatoid arthritis (primarily joint inflammation), insulin-dependent diabetes mellitus (caused by immune destruction of the insulin-secreting cells in the pancreas), haemolytic anaemia (premature destruction of red blood cells), and probably multiple sclerosis (destruction of myelin around nerves).

3. Antibodies inactivate pathogens in four main ways: **Neutralisation** describes the way in which antibodies bind to viral binding sites and bacterial toxins and stop their activity. Antibodies may also **inactivate particulate antigens**, such as bacteria, by sticking them together in clumps. Soluble antigens may be bound by antibodies and fall out of solution (**precipitation**) so that they lose activity. Antibodies also activate **complement** (a defence system involving serum proteins), tagging foreign cells so that they can be recognised and destroyed.

4. (a) **Phagocytosis**: Antibodies promote the formation of inactive clumps of foreign material that can easily be engulfed and destroyed by a phagocytic cell.

(b) **Inflammation**: Antibodies are involved in activation of complement (the defence system involving serum proteins which participate in the inflammatory response and other immune system activities).

(c) **Bacterial cell lysis**: Antibodies are involved in tagging foreign cells for destruction and in the activation of complement (the defence system involving serum proteins which participate in the lysis of foreign cells).

Vaccines and Vaccination (page 147)

1. **Attenuated viruses** are more effective in the long term because they tend to replicate in the body, and the original dose therefore increases over time. Such vaccines are derived from mutations accumulated over time in a laboratory culture, so there is always a risk

that they will back-mutate to a virulent form.

2. (a) High vaccination rates increase the rates of immunity within a population, so fewer people will contract the disease with each outbreak. Transmission of the disease is limited because there are fewer susceptible hosts for the disease to exploit, until eventually the disease no longer occurs in the population.

   (b) The success of the smallpox eradication programme was largely due to carefully monitored vaccination programmes together with strict surveillance of outbreaks which were then contained by isolating patients and even villages. Authorities responded quickly to investigate and limit outbreaks. In addition, humans were the only reservoir and there were no carriers, so it was easier to know when the disease was eradicated from a region.

   (c) Tuberculosis frequently remains dormant in infected people often for long periods of time, and only surfaces as active TB when their immune system is weakened. This means that it is difficult to locate all carriers of the disease and containment is not easily achievable without huge resources.

3. Several research institutions maintain the smallpox virus for ongoing research. Smallpox researchers must be vaccinated to prevent accidental contamination. More recently there have been concerns about the smallpox virus being used as a weapon in bioterrorism.

4. The number of reported cases of whooping cough increased significantly. They only began to drop again when vaccination rates increased again.

Monoclonal Antibodies (page 149)

1. B-lymphocytes.

2. Tumour cells are immortal and, when they fused with B lymphocytes, the resulting hybridomas acquire the ability to be cultured indefinitely.

3. Monoclonal antibodies produced using mouse (foreign) antibodies are likely to cause adverse immune reactions in some people. Newer methods include using genetic engineering techniques to selectively alter existing mouse antibodies to confer more human characteristics. Genetic engineering can also be used to construct chimaeric monoclonal antibodies using variable regions derived from mouse sources and constant regions derived from human sources. These techniques may produce monoclonal antibodies that are more compatible with the human immune system.

4. (a) Detection of bacteria or toxins in perishable food would allow the food to be disposed of rather than consumed and hence the possibility of food poisoning avoided.

   (b) Detection of pregnancy at home would give an instant result, and may circumvent a costly visit to a doctor until a pregnancy was confirmed. For some people, pregnancy detection in the privacy of their home is an attractive option.

   (c) Targeted treatment of cancerous tumours could avoid the need for more invasive or aggressive conventional cancer therapies (which have numerous, often distressing side effects).

Immunology and Public Health (page 151)

1. (a) Sporadic increases in incidence associated with seasonal changes.
   (b) Introduction of vaccination against this pathogen.

2. TB often remains dormant for long periods of time in people who are infected and shows no marked seasonality as with other diseases. Even when vaccination uptake goes up, this won't be immediately associated with a decline in disease incidence. Over a longer time period though, higher BCG vaccination rates are associated with a levelling off of TB incidence. Also, since the late 1990s, a decline in vaccine uptake has seen an increase in TB incidence.

3. 1990's spike in incidence represents an influenza epidemic and was most likely to be the result of an **antigenic shift** in the virus to which the human population had no immunity.

4. New strains of influenza arise each year, so public health authorities need to update their vaccine to match the currently circulating strain.

5. (a) The incidence of a disease, i.e. the number of new cases per unit time, is an important indicator to how aggressively a disease is spreading through a population. If new cases are appearing very rapidly, the measures required to control the disease (e.g. quarantine) will be different to those required if the disease was spreading slowly (e.g. vaccination).

   (b) The disease incidence data from the SARS outbreak indicated rapid spread from a focal point. This information enabled authorities to decide on an appropriate control programme involving quickly tracing sources of infection, effective quarantine and surveillance, and rapid implementation of hospital procedures and education campaigns aimed at halting spread of infection.

Antigenic Variability in Pathogens (page 153)

1. (a) The viral genome is contained on 8 short, loosely connected RNA segments. This enables ready exchange of genes between different viral strains and leads to alteration on the protein composition of the H and N glycoprotein spikes.

   (b) The body's immune system acquires antibodies to the H and N spikes (antigens) on the viral surface, but when different variants arise they are not recognized nor detected by the immune system (there is no immunological memory for the newly appearing antigens).

2. An antigenic shift represents the combination of two or more different viral strains in a new subtype with new properties and no immunological history in the population. Antigenic drifts are much smaller changes that occur continually over time and to which small adjustments are sufficient to provide resistance.

KEY TERMS: Word Find (page 154)

Q	I	B	J	I	I	M	I	T	R	M	S	E	A	H	H	Z	D	W	F	K	R	F	F	G
C	U	L	E	U	C	O	C	Y	T	E	S	E	N	K	A	G	M	G	G	G	F	L	P	U
K	C	Y	M	N	S	N	W	E	N	L	M	R	T	M	Y	D	A	F	Y	L	C	B	R	O
S	L	M	C	H	J	O	T	F	N	J	H	P	I	I	N	F	E	C	T	I	O	N	I	H
E	O	P	D	X	P	C	Y	Z	Y	F	V	P	G	Y	Y	I	T	R	O	O	Z	D	M	U
C	N	H	C	E	L	L	M	E	D	I	A	T	E	D	I	M	M	U	N	I	T	Y	A	M
O	A	O	Z	V	A	O	A	J	B	R	S	U	N	D	B	I	Q	T	W	R	G	N	R	O
N	L	C	U	A	S	N	N	I	P	A	S	S	I	V	E	I	M	M	U	N	I	T	Y	R
D	S	Y	M	C	M	A	T	Z	P	T	H	B	C	Y	Q	S	Q	X	L	V	S	V	R	A
A	E	T	F	C	A	L	I	I	U	N	Y	F	V	U	P	P	Z	V	L	O	S	R	E	L
R	L	E	B	I	C	A	B	X	Q	F	C	R	A	X	N	H	F	E	P	N	X	Y	S	I
Y	E	S	S	N	E	N	O	N	O	L	K	V	R	C	C	D	A	S	E	K	W	Y	P	M
R	C	S	D	A	L	T	D	L	R	A	L	N	I	U	F	V	O	G	A	P	T	F	O	M
E	T	B	A	T	L	I	I	W	W	M	N	B	A	S	P	Y	I	T	O	V	Y	M	N	U
S	I	M	Y	I	S	B	E	S	E	M	Q	S	B	X	S	T	J	Y	M	C	A	K	S	N
P	O	T	Q	O	R	O	S	K	S	A	X	T	I	I	N	T	E	F	I	O	Y	G	E	I
O	N	E	R	N	E	D	T	G	O	T	Y	H	L	A	P	Y	P	H	N	I	A	T	Y	T
N	S	V	B	O	M	I	A	C	T	I	V	E	I	M	M	U	N	I	T	Y	E	N	E	Y
S	I	Z	S	R	K	E	O	H	E	O	D	F	T	L	Y	M	P	H	O	C	Y	T	E	S
E	T	R	N	Z	Q	S	T	P	N	N	R	L	Y	N	N	O	I	Q	K	F	E	V	E	R

Variation (page 156)

1. Continuous variation is characterised by an exceedingly large number of phenotypic variations (so that a large sample of the population would exhibit a normal distribution for the trait in question). Such traits are determined by a large number of genes and are also frequently influenced by environment, e.g. hand span, weight, skin colour. Discontinuous variation is characterised by a limited number of phenotypic variants. Such traits are determined by a single gene and include features such as chin dimple (present/absent) and blood groups (A, B, AB, O).

2. (a) Wool production: Continuous
   (b) Hand span: Continuous
   (c) Blood groups: Discontinuous
   (d) Albinism: Discontinuous
   (e) Body weight: Continuous
   (f) Flower colour: Discontinuous

3. Environmental influence expected on: wool production (a), kernel colour (b), and body weight (e).

4. Student's own plot. Shape of the distribution is dependent on the data collected. The plot should show a **statistically normal distribution** if sample is representative of the population and large enough.
   (a) Calculations based on the student's own data.
   (b) Continuous distribution, normal distribution, or bell shaped curve are all acceptable answers if the data conform to this pattern.
   (c) Polygenic inheritance: Several (two or more) genes are involved in determining the phenotypic trait. Environment may also have an influence, especially if traits such as weight are chosen.
   (d) A large enough sample size (30+), selected randomly provides sufficient unbiased data to fairly indicate the distribution. The larger the sample size, the more closely one would expect the data plot to approximate the normal curve (assuming the sample was drawn from a population with a normal distribution for that attribute).

The Genome (page 159)

1. The **genome** of an organism is a complete haploid set of all chromosomes (i.e. all the genetic material carried by a single representative of each of all chromosome pairs).

2. (a) 5375 bases   (b) 5.375 kb   (c) 0.005375 Mb

3. 1542 bases

4. It is a comparatively small genome, others having 10 to 40 times as much genetic material (e.g. 48.6-190 kb).

Prokaryotic Chromosomes (page 160)

1. (a)-(c) any of in any order:
   - The prokaryotic chromosome is a singular circular chromosome. Eukaryote chromosomes comprise linear DNA packaged with proteins.
   - In prokaryotes, some genes are carried on extra-chromosomal plasmid DNA.
   - The prokaryote chromosome is attached to the plasma membrane and is not enclosed in a nuclear membrane (unlike the eukaryotic chromosomes).
   - Prokaryotic chromosomes consists almost entirely of protein coding genes and their regulatory sequences. Eukaryotic chromosomes contain much intronic DNA that does not code for proteins.

2. Because the DNA in prokaryotes is in direct contact with the cytoplasm, transcription (making mRNA) and translation (protein synthesis) can occur at the same time and the entire process of gene expression occurs much more rapidly than in eukaryotic cells, where the mRNA must leave the nucleus and enter the cytoplasm before translation can begin.

3. The bacterial genome (chromosome) is much smaller than the eukaryotic genome (all chromosomes).

Eukaryote Chromosome Structure (page 161)

1. (a) **DNA**: A long, complex nucleic acid molecule found in the chromosomes of nearly all organisms (some viruses have RNA instead). Provides the genetic instructions (genes) for the production of proteins and other gene products (e.g. RNAs).
   (b) **Chromatin**: Chromosomal material consisting of DNA, RNA, and histone and non-histone proteins. The term is used in reference to chromosomes in the non-condensed state.
   (c) **Histone**: Simple proteins that bind to DNA and help it to coil up during cell division. Histones are also involved in regulating DNA function in some way.
   (d) **Centromere**: A bump or constriction along the length of a chromosome to which spindle fibres attach during cell division. The centromere binds two chromatids together.
   (e) **Chromatid**: One of a pair of duplicated chromosomes produced prior to cell division, joined at the centromere. The terms chromatid and chromosome distinguish duplicated chromosomes before and after division of the centromere.

2. The chromatin (DNA and associated proteins) combine to coil up the DNA into a "super coiled" arrangement. The coiling of the DNA occurs at several levels. The DNA molecule is wrapped around bead-like cores of (8) histone proteins (called nucleosomes), which are

separated from each other by linker DNA sequences of about 50 bp. The histones (H1) are responsible for pulling nucleosomes together to form a 30 nm fibre. The chromatin fibre is then folded and wrapped so that it is held in a tight configuration. The different levels of coiling enables a huge amount of DNA to be packed, without tangling, into a very small space in a well organised, orderly fashion.

Nucleic Acids (page 163)

1. (a)-(e) See below (only half of the section of DNA illustrated in the workbook is shown here):

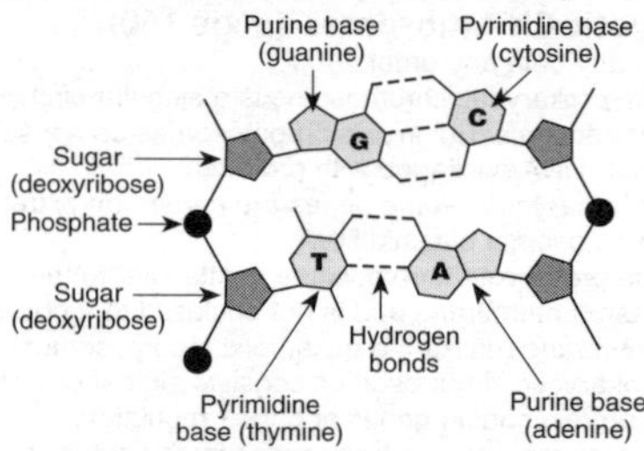

2. (a) The following bases always pair in a normal double strand of DNA:
   guanine with cytosine
   cytosine with guanine
   thymine with adenine
   adenine with thymine.
   (b) In mRNA, uracil replaces thymine in pairing with adenine.
   (c) The hydrogen bonds in double stranded DNA hold the two DNA strands together.

3. **Nucleotides** are building blocks of nucleic acids (DNA, RNA). Their precise sequence provides the genetic blueprint for the organism.

4. The **template strand** of DNA is complementary to the **coding strand** and provides the template for the transcription of the mRNA molecule. The coding strand has the same nucleotide sequence as the mRNA (it carries the code), except that thymine in the coding strand substitutes for uracil in the mRNA.

5.
	DNA	RNA
Sugar present	Deoxyribose	Ribose
Bases present	Adenine	Adenine
	Guanine	Guanine
	Cytosine	Cytosine
	Thymine	Uracil
Number of strands	Two (double)	One (single)
Relative length	Long	Short

Creating a DNA Model (page 165)

3. Labels as follows:

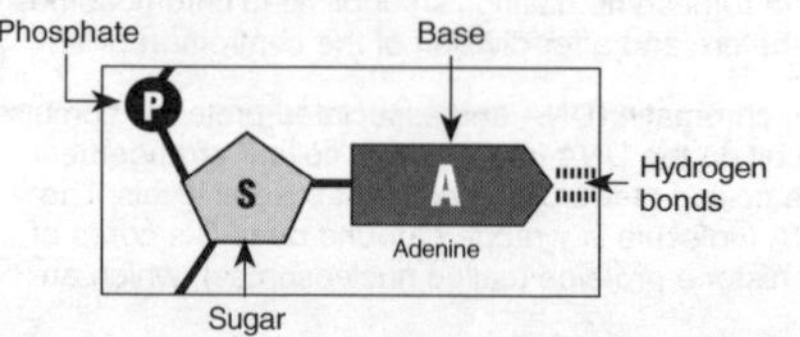

4. & 5.

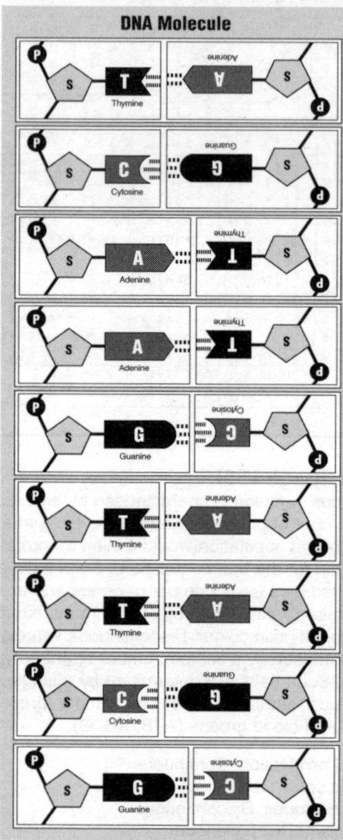

6. Factors that prevent a mismatch of nucleotides:
   – The number of hydrogen bond attraction points
   – The size (length) of the base (thymine and cytosine are short, adenine and guanine are long).
   Examples: Cytosine will not match cytosine because the bases are too far apart. Guanine will not match guanine because they are too long to fit side-by-side. Thymine will not match guanine because there is a mismatch in the number and orientation of H bonds.

DNA Molecules (page 169)

1. (a) 95 times more bps   (b) 630 times more bps

2. < 2% encodes proteins or structural RNA.

3. (a) Much of the once considered 'junk DNA' has now been found to give rise to functional RNA molecules (many with regulatory functions).
   (b) Complex organisms contain much more of this non-protein-coding DNA which suggests that these sequences contain RNA-only 'hidden' genes that have been conserved through evolution and have a definite role in the development of the organism.

The Genetic Code (page 170)

1. (a) DNA: ATG GGT TAC CTG AGG GTA ATA
                    CGG GCA CTT TAG
   (b) mRNA: AUG GGU UAC CUG AGG GUA AUA
                    CGG GCA CUU UAG
   Amino acids: Met Gly Tyr Leu Arg Val Iso
                Arg Ala Leu STOP

2. (a) Start: AUG   STOP: UAA, UAG, UGA
   (b) They indicate the starting and finishing points on the mRNA (as dictated by the DNA) for the instructions enabling the construction of a polypeptide chain.

The Simplest Case: Genes to Proteins
(page 171)

1. This exercise shows the way in which DNA codes for proteins. Nucleotide has no direct protein equivalent.
   (a) Triplet codes for amino acid.
   (b) Gene codes for polypeptide chain (may be a polypeptide, protein, or RNA product).
   (c) Transcription unit codes for functional protein.

2. (a) **Nucleotides** are made up of: Phosphate, sugar, and one of four bases (adenine, guanine, cytosine, and thymine or uracil).
   (b) **Triplet** is made up of three consecutive nucleotide bases that are read together as a code.
   (c) **Gene** comprises a sequence of triplets, starting with a start code and ending with a termination code.
   (d) **Transcription unit** is made up of two or more genes that together code for a functional protein.

3. Extra detail is provided; essential key words in bold. Steps in making a functional protein:
   • The template strand is made from the DNA coding strand and is transcribed into mRNA (**transcription**).
   • The code on the mRNA is translated into a sequence of amino acids (**translation**), which are linked with peptide bonds to form a polypeptide chain (this may be a functional protein in its own right).
   • The proteins coded by two or more genes come together to form the final functional protein (**folding into functional tertiary structure**).

Changes to the DNA Sequence (page 172)

1. Changes to the DNA base sequence can arise through unrepaired errors in transcription (these provide the background mutation rate) or by substances called mutagens which cause damage to DNA.

2. A mutation in a single base (e.g. a deletion or an insertion) can cause a frame shift, so that all subsequent codons are also changed. This generally results in a non-functional polypeptide, sometimes by creating a premature stop codon that halts translation.

3. The majority of mutations, especially in eukaryotes, are likely to be deleterious in that they usually alter the functional structure of an operational polypeptide (e.g the NSRD mutation). However, sometimes, especially in insects, bacteria, and viruses with very short generation times, mutations may arise that are beneficial in a certain selective environment (e.g. in an environment of heavy antibiotic use). Examples include:
   - Mutations in the genes coding for cell wall synthesis in bacteria which makes the wall less permeable to some (drug) molecules.
   - Mutations in the genes coding for the glycoprotein spikes in viruses. Changes enable them to evade the immune system of a naive host.

Meiosis (page 173)

1. In the first division of meiosis, homologous chromosomes pair to form bivalents. Segments of chromosome may be exchanged in crossing over and the homologues then separate (are pulled apart). This division reduces the number of chromosomes in the intermediate cells, so that only one chromosome from each homologous pair is present.

2. In the second division of meiosis, chromatids separate (are pulled apart), but the number of chromsomes stays the same. This is more or less a 'mitotic' division.

3. Mitosis involves a division of the chromatids into two new daughter cells thus maintaining the original number of chromosomes in the parent cell. Meiosis involves a division of the homologous pairs of chromosomes into two intermediary daughter cells thus reducing the diploid number by half. The second stage of meiosis is similar to a mitotic division, but the haploid number is maintained because the chromatids separate.

4. **A** shows metaphase of meiosis I; the homologous pairs of chromosomes are lined up on the cell equator. **B** shows metaphase of meiosis II; the individual chromatids are about to separate.

Crossing Over (page 175)

1. Unexpected combinations of alleles for genes will occur that would not normally be present in gametes.

2. Crossing over provides a source of increased genetic variation amongst individuals in a population. This is important for providing the raw material on which natural selection can act.

Crossing Over Problems (page 176)

Note that each of the problems is independent of the other problems (i.e. they are not a sequence).

1. (a) Gene sequences after crossing over at point 2:

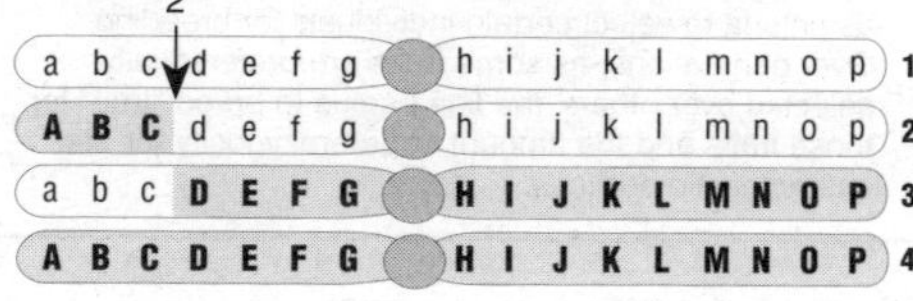

   (b) A, B, and C

2. (a) Gene sequences after crossing over at points 6 & 7.

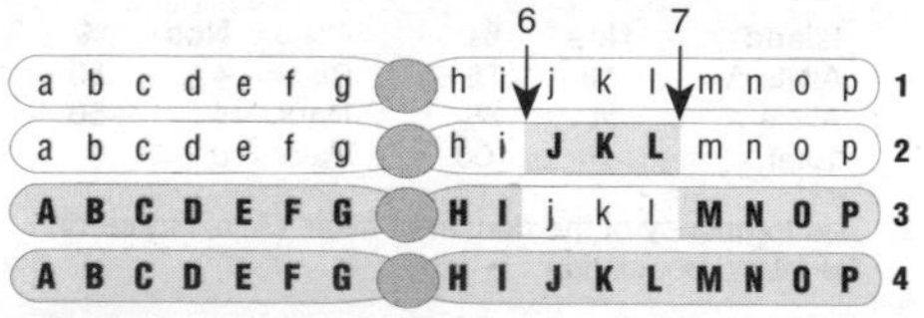

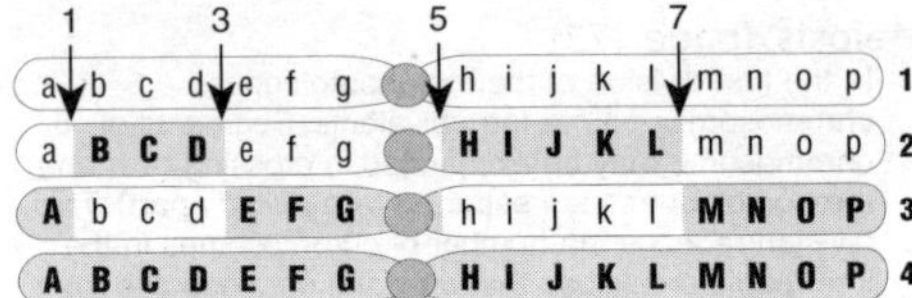

(b) J, K, and L

3. (a) Gene sequences after crossing over at points 1,3,5, and 7. Note that results for chromatids 2 & 3 are interchangeable.

1	3		5	7	
a	b c d	e f g	h i j k l	m n o p	1
a	**B C D**	e f g	**H I J K L**	m n o p	2
A	b c d	**E F G**	h i j k l	**M N O P**	3
A B C D		**E F G**	**H I J K L**	**M N O P**	4

(b) B, C, D and H, I, J, K, L

4. **Crossing over** increases the amount of mixing of genes to produce new combinations in offspring, therefore increases variation in the gene pool. It counteracts the effect of gene linkage.

KEY TERMS: Mix and Match (page 177)

Allele (CC), Amino acid (E), Base pairing rule (C), Chromatid (S), Chromosome (J), Condensation reaction (D), Diploid (G), DNA (AA), Gamete (B), Gene (BB), Genetic code (L), Haploid (I), Histones (K), Homologous chromosome (W), Hydrogen bonding (O), Independent assortment (H), Messenger RNA (A), Mutation (Q), Nucleic acid (Z), Nucelotides (M), Polypeptide (V), Protein (N), Protein synthesis (U), RNA (T), Somatic cells (P), Synapsis (X), Transcription (Y), Translation (R), Triplet code (F)

Genetic Diversity (page 179)

1. All dog breeds can interbreed to produce fertile offspring, therefore they constitute the same species.

2. The grey wolf is a highly variable species in many of its phenotypic characteristics (e.g. size fur thickness, fur colour). There is enough genetic diversity within the species to provide the basis for selection of particular traits. For example, coat colour is highly variable and provided enough diversity to produce the coat colours we see today in domestic dogs.

3. Specific desired traits (e.g. short dark coat) are used as criteria to select certain individuals for breeding. Over generations, as some traits are preferentially selected over others, the line begins to breed "true" for those traits and the amount of heterozygosity for the characteristic declines.

The Founder Effect (page 180)

1.

Mainland	Nos	%		Nos	%
Allele A	48	54.5	Black	11	25
Allele a	40	45.5	Dark	26	59
Total	88	100	Pale	7	16
Island	**Nos**	**%**		**Nos**	**%**
Allele A	12	75	Black	4	50
Allele a	4	25	Dark	4	50
Total	16	100	Pale	0	0

2. The frequency of the dominant allele (A) is higher on the island population.

---

3. (a) Plants: Seeds are carried by wind, birds and water.
   (b) Animals: Reach islands largely by 'rafting', whereby animals are carried offshore while clinging to vegetation; some animals survive better than others.
   (c) Non-marine birds: Blown off course and out to sea by a storm. Birds with strong stamina may survive.

4. Genetic drift: Small populations may suffer random, non-directional changes in the frequency of an allele.

Population Bottlenecks (page 181)

1. A sudden decrease in the size of a population can result in a corresponding reduction in genetic variation. This means the population has limited 'genetic resources' to cope with the selection pressures imposed on it. In particular, it is seen as reduced reproductive success and greater sensitivity to disease.

2. Poor genetic diversity means that if one individual is susceptible to a disease, then they are all likely to be vulnerable; a direct result of reduced genetic diversity.

3. With reduced genetic diversity, selection pressures acting on the population are likely to have devastating effects on survival if one trait is found to be unsuited. Since all cheetahs are virtually identical in their traits, if one individual is vulnerable to a selection pressure, then they will all succumb.

Genetic Drift (page 182)

1. **Genetic drift**: Random changes in allele frequencies in small isolated populations, owing to factors other than natural selection. Not all individuals, for various reasons, will be able to contribute their genes to the next generation.

2. Genetic drift reduces the amount of genetic variation in very small populations. Alleles may become eliminated altogether (0%) or become fixed (100%) as the only allele present in the gene pool for a particular gene.

3. Any endangered species with small numbers of individuals remaining: e.g. Puffin, monk seal, European lynx, otter, European beaver, hawksbill turtle, oryx, Siberian tiger (pop. ~500), Chinese tiger (pop. ~250), Sumatran tiger (pop. ~500), humpback whale, grey whale, blue whale.

Selective Breeding in Crop Plants (page 183)

1. A hybrid of inbred lines increases heterozygosity in the offspring. This is associated with a phenotypic response called hybrid vigour, characterised by greater adaptability, survival, growth, and fertility.

2. (a) Cauliflower: flowers
   (b) Kale: leaf
   (c) Broccoli: inflorescence
   (d) Brussels sprout: lateral buds
   (e) Cabbage: apical (terminal) bud
   (f) Kohlrabi: stem (swollen)

3. Any of the following:
   – High yielding crops to maximise crop production.
   – Disease and pest resistant crops lead to increased crop yields and require less pesticide/herbicide application so maximise profit.

    – Fast growing varieties enable the crops to be harvested more quickly and allow more crops to be planted and harvested in a season.

4. (a) Selective breeding for specific traits generally reduces genetic diversity by increasing homozygosity in the offspring. When selection in focussed on specific traits, other phenotypes (therefore genotypes) are rejected and their genes are lost from the gene pool. This is particularly the case when the genes for desirable traits are associated, e.g. a genotype for heavy fruiting might also be associated (e.g. through linkage) to lower seed production. Selection for one trait will then also select for another.

   (b) Retention of genetic diversity is particularly important in crop plants because it provides a pool of genes from which to improve strains and guard against loss of adaptability in crops. In terms of food security, it is dangerous to rely on only a restricted number of strains for most of our food. A good example is the Irish potato famine where potatoes were the main food crop and farmers relied almost exclusively on one high yielding potato variety. When this variety proved vulnerable to blight, most of the country's crop was lost and there was a huge famine. The country lost food security by relying on one variety and by not having a readily available store of diversity on which to draw.

Selective Breeding in Animals (page 185)

1. **Inbreeding** involves breeding between close relatives, and if practiced over a number of generations lead to increased homozygosity in a population. It is used by animal breeders to 'fix' desirable traits into a population, but an increase in the frequency of recessive, deleterious traits in homozygous form in a population can reduce the health and fitness and of a population and lower fertility levels. **Out-crossing** involves introducing new (unrelated) genetic material into a breeding line. It is used to increase the genetic diversity, and is used in line-breeding to restore vigour and fertility to a breeding line.

2. Assisted reproductive technologies, such as artificial insemination, cryopreservation, embryo transfer and *in vitro* fertilisation, are used routinely to produce large numbers of offspring with desirable traits (e.g. high growth rates or superior wool production). These techniques allow the desirable traits to be fixed more quickly into the population than would be possible from traditional selective breeding techniques.

3. Positive outcomes of selective breeding in domestic animals include; desirable traits are established within a relatively short period of time, breeders are able to produce animals with high growth rates, animals can be selected for which produce high yields of meat, wool, or milk, production of animals with good temperament, improve the birthing characteristics of a breed (e.g. easy calving), produce animals specifically suited to the climate or terrain.

Negative outcomes of selective breeding include; reduction of genetic variability can make the population susceptible to disease or physiological difficulties (e.g. hip displacement), fertility may decrease, the occurrence of deleterious genes becomes more widespread and the breed loses vigour.

4. Most genetic progress in dairy herds achieved by:
   (a) Selection of (and breeding from) high quality progeny from proven stock.
   (b) Extensive use of superior sires (breeding males) through artificial insemination.

5. **Genetic gain** refers to the gain towards a (reliably attained) desirable phenotype in a breed.

6. Mixed breeds combine the best of the characteristics of both species, i.e. optimum beef and milk production.

Darwin: Pigeon Fancier? (page 187)

1. Darwin was worried he would be ridiculed if he had no "experimental" evidence to support his theory that species could change over time. He saw the rapid changes achievable in pigeon breeds as good evidence for what could be achieved when a selection process was applied to populations.

2. A huge variety in pigeon morphology was generated by selective breeding from a generalised ancestor (the rock pigeon). These changes were not superficial, but extended to features of the skeleton too. Darwin suggested that, if such dramatic changes were achievable in a short time by a directed process, surely similarly large changes in morphology could occur over millions of years in natural populations subjected to different environments.

Haemoglobins (page 189)

1. (a) Respiratory pigments are able to bind reversibly with oxygen. They may bind and carry several oxygen molecules (and therefore increase the amount that can be carried over what can be dissolved in the plasma, which is very low).
   (b) The number of metal-containing prosthetic groups.

2. Organisms with a high metabolic activity (therefore high oxygen demand) have haemoglobins with a greater oxygen carrying capacity (values are highest in endothermic homeotherms, i.e. birds and mammals).

3. Large molecular weight respiratory pigments are too large to be held within cells and must be carried dissolved in the plasma.

4. Haemoglobin binds oxygen reversibly, taking up oxygen when oxygen tensions are high (lungs), carries oxygen to where it is required (the tissues) and releases it.

5. (a) As oxygen level in the blood increases, more oxygen combines with haemoglobin. However, the relationship is not linear: Hb saturation remains high even when blood oxygen levels fall very low.
   (b) When oxygen level (partial pressure) in the blood or tissues is low, haemoglobin saturation declines markedly and oxygen is released (to the tissues).

6. (a) Foetal Hb has a higher affinity for oxygen than adult Hb (it can carry 20-30% more oxygen).
   (b) This higher affinity is necessary because it enables oxygen to pass from the maternal Hb to the foetal Hb across the placenta.

7. (a) The Bohr effect
   (b) Actively respiring tissue (especially tissue with high metabolic demand, such as working muscle) consumes a lot of oxygen and generates a lot of carbon dioxide. This lowers tissue (blood) pH causing more oxygen to be released from the haemoglobin to where it is required.

8. Myoglobin preferentially picks up oxygen from Hb and is able to act as an oxygen store in the muscle.

Starch, Cellulose, and Cell Walls (page 191)

1. Cellulose is a linear molecule consisting of several hundred to several thousand β-glucose molecules bonded by a 1,4 glycosidic bond. Starch is composed of two main molecules; amylose which forms a helix, and a branched molecule, amylopectin. Amylose consists of α-glucose monomers bonded by 1-4 glycosidic bonds. Amylopectin also consists of α-glucose monomers, but around 4% of its bonds are 1,6 glycosidic bonds, which causes it to branch.

2. Cellulose has a structural role, providing strength and support to the plant cell. Starch provides the plant with a means of storing energy. Glucose molecules are stored as starch inside amyloplasts in a compact form which can be easily hydrolysed to be released as an energy source when required.

3. The lattice structure of the cells in wood provide a low density structure while the cellulose (making up 50% of wood) provides strength.

4. Cellulose microfibrils are composed of molecules that possess strong intramolecular bonds (covalent bonds) as well as having strong hydrogen bonding between cellulose molecules.

5. (a) ~650 MPa
   (b) ~540 MPa
   (c) ~140 MPa
   (d) ~ 620 MPa

Chloroplasts (page 193)

1. (a) Stroma
   (b) Stroma lamellae
   (c) Outer membrane
   (d) Granum
   (e) Thylakoid
   (f) Inner membrane

2. Chloroplasts are primarily concentrated in the loosely packed mesophyll tissue, where there is the best access to light through the transparent, thin leaf blade. The structure of the chloroplasts themselves also aids light capture. The thylakoid membranes containing the chlorophyll, are organised in stacks, spaced apart by lamellae to maximise efficiency of function. This arrangement maximises the amount of chlorophyll-containing membranes within the organelle.

3. A Cell wall supports the cell and limits its volume.
   B Chloroplasts plastids containing the pigment chlorophyll, in which photosynthesis takes place.

DNA Replication is Semi-Conservative (page 194)

1. Generation 1 consisted of only intermediate DNA. This ruled out the conservative method where equal quantities of heavy and light DNA would be expected. Generation 2 produced light and intermediate DNA in equal amounts. This ruled out the dispersive method which would produce a single type of DNA that would separate out somewhere between the intermediate and light bands.

2. (a) Conservative
   (b) Dispersive

DNA Replication (page 195)

1. DNA replication prepares a chromosome for cell division by producing two chromatids which are (or should be) identical copies of the genetic information for the chromosome.

2. (a) Step 1: Enzymes unwind DNA molecule to expose the two original strands.
   (b) Step 2: DNA polymerase enzyme uses the two original strands as templates to make complementary strands.
   (c) Step 3: The two resulting double-helix molecules coil up to form two chromatids in the chromosome.

3. (a) **Helicase**: Unwinds the 'parental' strands.
   (b) **DNA polymerase I**: Hydrolyses the RNA primer and replaces it with DNA.
   (c) **DNA polymerase III**: Elongates the leading strand. It synthesises the new Okazaki fragment until it encounters the primer on the previous fragment.
   (d) **Ligase**: Joins Okazaki fragments into a continuous length of DNA.

4. 16 minutes 40 seconds
   4 million nucleotides replicated at the rate of 4000 per second: $4\,000\,000 \div 4000 = 1000$ s
   Convert to minutes $= 1000 \div 60 = 16.67$ minutes
   (Note that, under ideal conditions, most of a bacteria's cell cycle is spent in cell division).

Does DNA Really Carry the Code? (page 197)

1. A- Griffith first injected disease causing bacteria into healthy mice to confirm the action of the bacteria. The bacteria were then heated to kill them and injected into healthy mice. M- These mice did not develop pneumonia confirming it was the living bacteria that was causing the disease.

2. A- Sulfur is found in proteins but not in DNA (or to a much lesser extent) while phosphorus is found in DNA but not proteins. M- If the sulfur was found in the infected bacteria then the proteins carried the genetic information. If phosphorus was found then it was the DNA that carried the information.

3. A- This shows that the result is not peculiar to, or the result of, the experiment itself. M- Rather it is a property of the system being studied.

Mitosis and the Cell Cycle (page 198)
1. Mitosis produces two identical cells from a parent cell.

2. Chromosome replication, which occurs in interphase, describes the replication of the DNA so that there are two copies of all the genetic material. Mitosis describes division of the nucleus and cytokinesis describes division of the cytoplasm. Cell division includes both mitosis and cytokinesis.

3. Homologous chromosomes are chromosome pairs of the same length, centromere position, and staining pattern with genes for the same characteristics at corresponding loci. A chromatid is one of the two identical copies of DNA making up a duplicated chromosome, which are joined at their centromeres.

Understanding Mitosis (page 199)
1. A. Anaphase
   B. Prophase
   C. Late metaphase (early anaphase is also acceptable).
   D. Late anaphase
   E. Cytokinesis (late telophase is also acceptable).

2. Replicate the DNA to form a second chromatid. Coil up into visible chromosomes to avoid tangling.

3. In plant cells, there are no centrioles and the centrosome form the spindle. In plants, the division of the cytoplasm involves the formation of a cell plate where the new cell wall will form. In animal cells, the division of the cytoplasm occurs earlier and does not involve the formation of a cell plate (so it is quicker).

4. A. Interphase: The stage between cell divisions (mitoses). Just before mitosis, the DNA is replicated to form an extra copy of each chromosome (still part of the same chromosome as an extra chromatid).
   B. Late prophase: Chromosomes condense (coil and fold up) into visible form. Centrioles move to opposite ends of the cell.
   C. Metaphase: Spindle fibers form between the centrioles. Chromosomes attach to the spindle fibers at the cell 'equator'.
   D. Late anaphase: Chromatids from each chromosome are pulled apart and move in opposite directions, towards the centrioles.
   E. Telophase: Chromosomes begin to unwind again. Two new nuclei form. The cell plate forms across the midline where the new cell wall will form.
   F. Cytokinesis: Cell cytoplasm divides to create two distinct 'daughter cells' from the original cell. It is in this form for most of its existence, and carries out its designated role (normal function).

5. Mitotic cell division is required for:
   - Growth, resulting in increase in the size of the organism.
   - Repair of tissues for the replacement of damaged or loss tissues.
   - Reproduction for asexual reproduction in some simple organisms, e.g. yeasts.

6. (a) A plant: Meristematic tissues (root and shoot tip and the vascular cambium).
   (b) A mammal: Undifferentiated epithelial cells (e.g. cheek cells, cells lining the gut, skin cells) and the stem cells that give rise to the blood cells.

7. Mitosis produces two cells identical to the single parent cell. In contrast, meiosis produces haploid cells, with a reassorted combination of alleles.

The Cell Cycle and Cancer (page 201)
1. Exposure to carcinogens can damage the DNA and trigger uncontrolled cell division (and tumour formation).

2. A single cause of cancer can be difficult to pin-point because there are many factors (environmental, lifestyle, genetic, and ageing) which can interact and result in the development of a cancer.

Differentiation of Human Cells (page 202)
1. An undifferentiated cell can potentially give rise to any cell type but, as a cell differentiates, some genes get switched on while others get switched off, and the cell takes on a specialised role. Different cell types have different genes switched on or off, hence the large number of cell types.

2. The switching on or off of genes during cellular differentiation is permanent and, once this has happened, the cell's fate becomes determined and it cannot 'back-track' along its developmental path.

Human Cell Specialisation (page 203)
(b) **Erythrocyte**:
   Features: Biconcave cell, lacking mitochondria, nucleus, and most internal membranes. Contains the oxygen-transporting pigment, haemoglobin.
   Role: Uptake, transport, and release of oxygen to the tissues. Some transport of CO_2. Lack of organelles creates more space for oxygen transport. Lack of mitochondria prevents oxygen use.
(c) **Retinal rod (photoreceptor) cell**:
   Features: Long, narrow cell with light-sensitive pigment (rhodopsin) embedded in the membranes.
   Role: Detection of light: light causes a structural change in the membranes and leads to a nerve impulse (result is visual perception).
(d) **Skeletal muscle cell**:
   Features: Cylindrical shape with banded myofibrils. Capable of contraction (shortening).
   Role: Move voluntary muscles acting on skeleton.
(e) **Intestinal goblet cell (secretory cell)**:
   Features: Flask-shaped cell with basal nucleus and a cell interior filled with mucus globules.
   Role: Secrete mucus to protect the epithelium from abrasion and from the action of digestive enzymes.
(f) **Motor neurone cell**:
   Features: Cell body with a long extension (the axon) ending in synaptic bodies. Axon is insulated with a sheath of fatty material (myelin).
   Role: Rapid conduction of motor nerve impulses from the spinal cord to effectors (e.g. muscle).
(g) **Spermatocyte**:
   Features: Motile, flagellated cell with mitochondria. Nucleus forms a large proportion of the cell.
   Role: Male gamete for sexual reproduction. Mitochondria provide the energy for motility.
(h) **Osteocyte**:
   Features: Cell with calcium matrix around it. Fingerlike extensions enable the cell to be supplied

with nutrients and wastes to be removed.
Role: In early stages, secretes the matrix that will be the structural component of bone. Provides strength.

Differentiation of Plant Cells (page 204)

1. The meristems in plants consist of undifferentiated cells and cell division in the meristems provide new cells for expansion and differentiation of tissues.

2. Primary meristems are located in apical regions, i.e. the growing tips of the shoots and roots. Primary meristems are responsible for an increase in length or height. Some plants also have secondary meristems (the vascular cambium) encircling the stem, which produces increase in plant girth (diameter).

3. Meristematic tissue comprises undifferentiated cells (it is equivalent to stem cells in animals).

4. Primary tissues are formed from the primary meristems. Three primary meristems are produced from the apical meristem. The protoderm forms the epidermis, the ground meristem forms pith, cortex, and mesophyll, while the procambium leads to the formation of primary phloem and xylem. These form vascular bundles.

Plant Cell Specialisation (page 205)

1. (b) **Pollen grain**:
   Features: Small, lightweight, often with spikes.
   Role: houses male gamete for sexual reproduction.
   (c) **Palisade parenchyma cell**:
   Features: Column-shaped cell with chloroplasts.
   Role: Primary photosynthetic cells of the leaf.
   (d) **Epidermal cell**:
   Features: Waxy surface on a flat-shaped cell.
   Role: Provides a barrier to water loss on leaf.
   (e) **Vessel element**:
   Features: Rigid remains of a dead cell. No cytoplasm. End walls perforated. Walls are strengthened with lignin fibres.
   Role: Rapid conduction of water through the stem. Provides support for stem/trunk.
   (f) **Stone cell**:
   Features: Very thick lignified cell wall inside the primary cell wall. The cytoplasm is restricted to a small central region of the cell.
   Role: Protection of the seed inside the fruit.
   (g) **Sieve tube member**:
   Features: Long, tube-shaped cell without a nucleus. Cytoplasm continuous with other sieve cells above and below it. Cytoplasmic streaming is evident.
   Role: Responsible for translocation of sugars etc.
   (h) **Root hair cell**:
   Features: Thin cuticle with no waxy layer. High surface area relative to volume.
   Role: Facilitates the uptake of water and ions.

Root Cell Development (page 206)

1. (a) Cells specialise to take on specific functions.
   (b) Cells are becoming longer and/or larger.
   (c) Cells are dividing by mitosis.

2. (a) Late anaphase; chromatids are being pulled apart and are at opposite poles.
   (b) Telophase; there are two new nuclei formed and the

cell plate is visible.
   (c) 25 of 250 cells were in mitosis, therefore mitosis occupies 25/250 or one tenth of the cell cycle.

3. The **cambium layer** of cells (lying under the bark between the outer phloem layer of cells and the inner xylem layer of cells). **Note**: Cells dividing from each side of this layer specialise to form new phloem on the outside and new xylem on the inside.

Levels of Organisation (page 207)

1. **Animals**
   (a) **Molecular**: Adrenaline, collagen, DNA, phospholipid
   (b) **Organelles**: Lysosome, ribosomes
   (c) **Cells**: Leucocyte, mast cell, neurone, Schwann cell
   (d) **Tissues**: Blood, bone, cardiac muscle, cartilage, squamous epithelium
   (e) **Organs**: Brain, heart, spleen
   (f) **Organ system**: Nervous system, reproductive system

2. **Plants**
   (a) **Molecular**: Pectin, cellulose, DNA, phospholipid
   (b) **Organelles**: Chloroplasts, ribosomes
   (c) **Cells**: Companion cells, epidermal cell, fibres, tracheid
   (d) **Tissues**: Collenchyma*, mesophyll, parenchyma*, phloem, sclerenchyma
   (e) **Organs**: Flowers, leaf, roots
   * **Note**: Parenchyma and collenchyma are simple tissues comprising only one type of cell (parenchyma and collenchyma cells respectively). Simple plant tissues are usually identified by cell name alone.

Animal Tissues (page 208)

1. The organisation of cells into specialised tissues allows the tissues to perform particular functions. This improves efficiency of function because different tasks can be shared amongst specialised cells. Energy is saved in not maintaining non-essential organelles in cells that do not require them.

2. (a) **Epithelial tissues**: Single or multiple layers of simple cells forming the lining of internal and external body surfaces. Cells rest on a basement membrane of fibers and collagen and may be specialised. **Note**: epithelial cells may be variously shaped: squamous (flat), cuboidal, columnar etc.
   (b) **Nervous tissue**: Tissue comprising densely packed nerve cells specialised for transmitting electro-chemical impulses. Nerve cells may be associated with supportive cells (e.g. Schwann cells), connective tissue, and blood vessels.
   (c) **Muscle tissue**: Dense tissue comprising highly specialized contractile cells called fibers held together by connective tissues.
   (d) **Connective tissues**: Supporting tissue of the body, comprising cells widely dispersed in a semi-fluid matrix (or fluid in the case of blood and lymph).

3. (a) Muscle tissue is made up of long muscle fibre cells made up of myofibrils. The myofibrils are made up of contractile proteins actin and myosin, which cause the muscle fibres to contact when stimulated. The contraction results in movement of the organism itself (locomotion) or movement of an internal organ.
   (b) Nervous tissue comprises two main tissue types: neurones which transmit nerve signals and glial

cells which provide support to the neurones. Neurones have several protrusions (dendrites or axons) from their cell body which allow conduction of nerves impulses to target cells.

Plant Tissues (page 209)

1. **Collenchyma**
   Cell type(s): collenchyma cells
   Role: provides flexible support.
   Sclerenchyma
   Cell type(s): sclerenchyma cells
   Role: provides rigid, hard support.

   Root Endodermis
   Cell type(s): endodermal cells
   Role: Provides selective barrier regulating the passage of substances from the soil to the vascular tissue.

   Pericycle
   Cell type(s): parenchyma cells
   Role: Production of branch roots, synthesis and transport of alkaloids.

   Leaf mesophyll
   Cell type(s): spongy mesophyll, palisade mesophyll
   Role: Main photosynthesis site in the plant.

   Xylem
   Cell type(s): tracheids, vessel members, fibers, paraenchyma cells
   Role: Conducts water and dissolved minerals in vascular plants.

   Phloem
   Cell type(s): sieve-tube members, companion cells, parenchyma, fibers, sclereids
   Role: transport of dissolved organic material (including sugars) within vascular plants.

   Epidermis
   Cell type(s): epidermal cells, guard cells, subsidiary cells, and epidermal hairs (trichomes).
   Role: Protection against water loss, regulation of gas exchange, secretion, water and mineral absorption.

KEY TERMS: Word Find (page 210)

```
I  M  T  W  H  O  M  O  L  O  G  O  U  S  C  H  R  O  M  O  S  O  M  E  S
I  A  Z  K  G  F  M  Q  H  T  X  I  B  O  L  H  V  C  I  C  E  E  Y  T  D
R  S  R  T  L  T  A  M  I  V  R  Y  T  J  G  G  L  Y  C  O  G  E  N  J  X
D  V  U  A  N  A  P  H  A  S  E  I  E  N  T  T  I  S  S  U  E  N  Z  J  G
N  A  H  P  W  T  P  H  L  O  E  M  C  E  N  T  R  I  O  L  E  S  Q  D  F
A  G  W  A  D  P  H  N  U  C  L  E  A  R  E  N  V  E  L  O  P  E  D  N  X
P  C  F  H  A  E  M  O  G  L  O  B  I  N  L  O  R  J  J  Y  Z  S  Q  V  T
O  A  K  M  U  A  N  U  M  I  T  O  S  I  S  R  J  A  D  V  L  U  Q  N  H
L  N  L  R  D  N  W  G  F  Y  P  R  O  P  H  A  S  E  H  H  D  W  Z  F  L
Y  C  J  U  S  Q  K  B  N  R  I  M  E  T  A  P  H  A  S  E  R  L  D  P  A
M  E  C  Y  T  O  K  I  N  E  S  I  S  D  K  R  S  T  A  R  C  H  K  E  K
E  R  T  E  L  O  P  H  A  S  E  C  V  C  H  L  O  R  O  P  L  A  S  T  O
R  B  A  Y  I  A  P  N  D  N  A  R  E  P  L  I  C  A  T  I  O  N  A  Y  I
A  N  S  T  R  O  M  A  T  A  L  W  X  M  O  H  A  P  L  O  I  D  N  Q  D
S  Y  T  P  J  A  G  W  N  K  O  C  C  E  L  L  U  L  O  S  E  R  N  K  U
E  P  O  R  G  A  N  S  Y  O  K  T  H  C  G  D  C  E  L  L  C  Y  C  L  E
N  I  C  E  L  L  U  L  A  R  D  I  F  F  E  R  E  N  T  I  A  T  I  O  N
```

Transport and Exchange Systems (page 212)

1. Diffusion is too inefficient and slow to provide (and remove) materials (wastes, oxygen, nutrients) quickly enough to and from all the cells of larger animals. Instead, organs specialised to perform certain "exchange tasks", such as lungs and kidneys, are required and these are associated with transport mechanisms (e.g. circulatory system) to move the materials to exchange sites.

2. (a) Materials move by bulk (mass) flow in the circulatory system of a vertebrate.
   (b) Materials move by diffusion in flatworms/unicells.
   (c) Any two of: lungs or gills, gut, kidneys.

Surface Area and Volume (page 213)

1.

Cube	Surface Area	Volume	Ratio
3 cm:	3 x 3 x 6 = 54	3 x 3 x 3 = 27	2.0 to 1
4 cm:	4 x 4 x 6 = 96	4 x 4 x 4 = 64	1.5 to 1
5 cm:	5 x 5 x 6 = 150	5 x 5 x 5 = 125	1.2 to 1

2. Surface area to volume graph: see the next column:

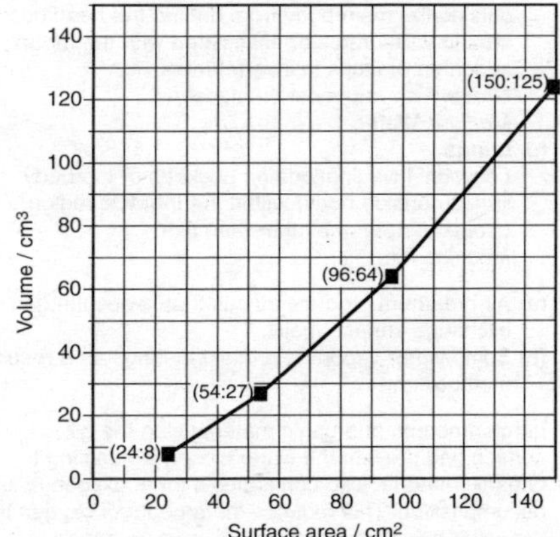

3. Volume

4. Increasing size leads to less surface area for a given volume. The surface area to volume ratio decreases.

5. Less surface area at the cell surface. This is the gas exchange surface, so large cells will have difficulty moving enough materials in and out of the cell to meet demands. This is what limits a cell's maximum size.
   Note: Eukaryote cells are typically about 0.01-0.1 mm in size, but some can be bigger than 1 mm. The largest cell is the female sex cell (ovum) of the ostrich, which averages 15-20 cm in length. Technically a single cell, it is atypical in size because almost the entire mass of the egg is food reserve in the form of yolk, which is not part of the functioning structure of the cell itself.

Gas Exchange in Animals (page 215)

1. (a) Provides adequate supply and removal of respiratory gases necessary for an active (metabolically demanding) lifestyle.

(b) Enables animals to attain a larger size (as they are freed from a dependence on direct diffusion of gases across thin body surfaces).

2. (a) The air sacs function in ventilating the lungs (where gas exchange takes place). They facilitate one way (rather than to and fro) flow of air through the lungs.
   (b) Birds require an efficient gas exchange system because of their high metabolic rate (associated with flight). However they do not want to carry a large amount of lung tissue because this would be heavy and hinder flight (hence air sacs).

3. (a) **Body surface**
   Location: The entire body surface is involved.
   Group: Characteristic of small and/or thin animals, e.g. cnidarians, ctenophores, annelids, flatworms.
   Medium: Air (in damp environments) or water.
   (b) **Tracheal tubes**
   Location: Thin tubes extend inwards from spiracles at the body surface located on the abdomen.
   Group: Insects and some spiders.
   Medium: Air.
   (c) **Gills**
   Location: Thin, filamentous structures that extend outside the main body from behind the head/buccal area in vertebrates or associated with the thorax, abdomen or limbs in invertebrates.
   Group: Fish and most crustaceans.
   Medium: Water.
   (d) **Lungs**
   Location: Invaginations (in-pockets) of the body surface (inside body) within the thoracic region.
   Group: Vertebrates other than fish.
   Medium: Air.

4. (a) Air breathers produce mucus that keeps the gas exchange surface moist.
   (b) Some water vapour is present in lungs as a result of metabolism.

5. Large amounts of organic material clog the gill surface and prevent the water closely contacting it. Organic material also consumes a lot of oxygen in its decomposition. This reduces the amount of oxygen in the water available to animals for gas exchange.

6. An animal's gas exchange system must be appropriate to the environment in which it must operate. Gills do not function in air because the gill tissue needs to be supported by the water to prevent its collapse in the less dense medium of air. In air, the gill tissue rapidly dries out and, once dry, the surface will not operate effectively for gas exchange. In water, lungs do not function because water is too dense a medium to enter and leave an internalised structure. The tracheae of insects operate well in terrestrial organisms of a small size because they can provide oxygen directly to the tissues. With direct oxygen delivery, a respiratory pigment in the blood is not required. In aquatic insects, the tracheae extend into flattened gills on the abdomen, and these increase oxygen uptake from the water, where oxygen extraction is more difficult than in air (because diffusion rates are slower).

Gas Exchange in Insects (page 217)

1. **Simple explanation**: In insect tracheae, gases move by diffusion directly into the tissues. Gases diffuse into and out of the fluid at the end of the tracheole, and the fluid acts as the medium for gas exchange into the tissues. **Detailed explanation**: At rest, the fluid moves into the tracheoles, oxygen diffuses into the fluid and CO_2 diffuses out. When the muscles contract, the fluid is drawn into the tissues, and oxygen can diffuse into the tissues while CO_2 diffuses out into the fluid.

2. Valves present in the spiracles control the rate of entry and exit of air into and out of the tracheal system. This enables the rate of gas exchange to be regulated according to the changing activity levels (and therefore gas exchange requirements) of the insect.

3. Ventilation occurs when the insect makes rhythmic body movements helping to move the air in and out of the tracheae.

4. Tracheal systems provide direct delivery of oxygen to the tissues, without relying on a circulatory fluid combined with a respiratory pigment. This system is rapid and efficient for small sized organisms and has the advantage of reducing the reliance of insects on water (water is a necessity for organisms relying on diffusion across a moist body surface). A reduced dependence on freely available water has allowed insects to colonise some of the driest, most inhospitable places on Earth.

Gas Exchange in Aquatic Insects (page 218)

1. (a)-(c) any of, in any order:
   - Tracheal gills increase surface area for gas exchange, e.g. aquatic insect larvae such as mayfly larvae. Note that the anal and caudal "gills" of some aquatic insects are often involved in osmoregulation.
   - Trapped air beneath the wings provides an oxygen store above the spiracles, e.g. *Dytiscus*.
   - A plastron formed by a layer of air trapped against the spiracles by hydrofuge hairs. A plastron forms a non-compressible gill into which gases can diffuse, e.g. adult hydrophilid beetles.
   - Siphons to the water surface provide a link between the spiracles and the air above, e.g. mosquito larvae.

2. Physiological adaptation: Presence of a respiratory pigment (haemoglobin) either in the blood (*Chironomus*) or in the abdomen (*Anisops*).

Gas Exchange in Fish (page 219)

1. (a)-(c) any of, in any order:
   - Greatly folded surface of gills (high surface area).
   - Gills supported and kept apart from each other by the gas exchange medium (water).
   - Water flow across the gill surface is opposite to that of the blood flow in the gill capillaries (countercurrent), facilitating oxygen uptake.
   - Pumping mechanism of operculum aids movement of the water across the gas exchange surface.

2. (a) As blood flows through the gill capillaries (gaining oxygen) it encounters blood of increasing oxygen content, so a diffusion gradient is maintained across the entire gill surface.
   (b) Parallel flow would result in rapid equilibration of

oxygen saturation between the blood and the water and diffusion into the blood would stop.

3. (a) **Ventilation**: Moving water across the gill surface.
   (b) Ventilation prevents stagnation of the water at the gill surface and maintains the concentration gradient necessary for continued gas exchange.
   (c) **Pumping**: Operculum acts as a pump, drawing water past the gill filaments.
   Continuous swimming: Continuous (usually rapid) swimming with the mouth open produces a constant flow of water over the gill filaments.
   (d) These fish rely on being able to swim rapidly and continuously to provide the necessary ventilation of their gill surfaces. If they do not have the room to do this they will asphyxiate and die.

4. Oxygen availability in water is low anyway, so anything that lowers this still further (high temperature of decomposition of organic material) increases the vulnerability of fish to oxygen deprivation. This is especially so for fish with high oxygen requirements such as trout and salmon.

Stomata and Gas Exchange (page 221)

1. (a) and (b) Any two of:
   - Thin blade to maximise the surface area for light capture and gas exchanges.
   - Loosely packed mesophyll facilitates gas movements into and out of the leaf.
   - Transparent so there is no impairment to light entry.
   - Waterproof cuticle reduces transpirational water losses.

2. (a) Net gas exchange (no photosynthesis): net use of oxygen and net production of carbon dioxide.
   (b) Net gas exchange (photosynthesis): net use of carbon dioxide and net production of oxygen.

3. (a) Facilitate diffusion of gases into and out of the leaf.
   (b) Provide a large surface area for gas exchanges (around the cell.

4. Stomata regulate the entry and exit of gases into and out of the leaf (they also regulate water loss).

5. (a) **Stomatal opening**: Active transport of potassium ions into the guard cells (which lowers the water potential of the guard cells) is followed by osmotic influx of water. This causes the guard cells to swell and become turgid. The structure of the guard cell walls causes them to buckle out, opening the stoma.
   (b) **Stomatal closure**: Potassium ions leave the guard cell (making the water potential of the guard cells less negative) and water follows by osmosis. The guard cells become flaccid and sag together closing the stoma.

Adaptations of Xerophytes (page 223)

1. **Xeromorphic** adaptations allow xerophytes to survive and grow in areas with low or irregular water supplies.

2. (a)-(c), three in any order:
   - Modification of leaves to reduce transpirational loss (e.g. spines, curling, leaf hairs).
   - Shallow, but extensive fibrous root system to extend area from which water is taken and to take advantage of overnight condensation.
   - Water storage in stems or leaves.
   - Rounded, squat shape of plant body to reduce surface area for water loss.

3. The CAM metabolism (found only in xerophytic plants, many of which are succulents) allows carbon dioxide to be fixed during the dark. This produces organic acids which accumulate in the leaves and later release carbon dioxide into the Calvin cycle during daylight (when light energy is available to provide H^+ and ATP for photosynthesis). The stomata can then stay closed during the day when transpirational losses are highest.

4. A moist microenvironment reduces the gradient in water potential between the leaf and the air, so there is less tendency for water to leave the plant.

5. In a high salt environment, free water is scarce. Sea shoreline plants (halophytes) therefore have many xeromorphic adaptations.

Mammalian Transport (page 225)

1. (a) Head   (d) Gut (intestines)
   (b) Lungs   (e) Kidneys
   (c) Liver   (f) Genitals/lower body

Arteries (page 226)

1. (a) Tunica externa   (c) Endothelium
   (b) Tunica media   (d) Blood (or lumen)

2. (a) Thick, elastic walls can withstand the high pressure of the blood being pumped from the heart. **Note**: Elasticity also helps to even out the surges that occur with each contraction of the heart. This keeps the blood moving forward in a continuous flow.
   (b) Blood pressure is low within the arterioles.

3. The smooth muscle around arteries helps to regulate blood flow and pressure. By contracting or relaxing it alters the diameter of the artery and adjusts the volume of blood as required.

4. (a) The diameter of the artery increases.
   (b) The blood pressure decreases.

Veins (page 227)

1. (a) Veins have less elastic and muscle tissue than arteries.
   (b) Veins have a larger lumen than arteries.

2. Most of the structural differences between arteries and veins are related to the different blood pressures inside the vessels. Blood in veins travels at low pressure and veins do not need to be as strong, hence the thinner layers of muscle and elastic tissue and the relatively larger lumen. **Note**: There is still enough elastic and muscle tissue to enable the veins to adjust to changes in blood volume and pressure.

3. Veins are "massaged" by the skeletal muscles (e.g. leg muscles). Valves (together with these muscular movements) help to return venous blood to the heart by preventing backflow away from the heart.
   Extra note: When skeletal muscles contract and tighten around a vein the valves open and blood is driven towards the heart. When the muscles relax, the valves close, preventing backflow.

4. Venous blood oozes out in an even flow from a wound because it has lost a lot of pressure after passing through the narrow capillary vessels (with their high resistance to flow). Arterial blood spurts out rapidly because it is being pumped directly from the heart and has not yet entered the capillary networks.

Capillaries (page 228)

1. **Capillaries** are very small blood vessels forming networks or beds that penetrate all parts of the body. The only tissue present is an endothelium of squamous epithelial cells. In contrast, **arteries** have a thin endothelium, a central layer of elastic tissue and smooth muscle and a thick outer layer of elastic and connective tissue. **Veins** have a thin endothelium, a central layer of elastic and muscle tissue and a thin outer layer of elastic connective tissue. In addition, veins also have valves.

2. (a) Sinusoids differ from capillaries in that they are wider and follow a more convoluted path through the tissue. They are lined with phagocytic cells rather than the usual endothelial lining of capillaries.
   (b) Capillaries and sinusoids are similar in that they both transport blood from arterioles to venules.

Capillary Networks (page 229)

1. Capillaries are branching networks of fine blood vessels where exchanges between blood and tissue take place. Blood enters the network at the arteriolar end and is collected by venues at the venous end. The true capillaries form a network outside of the vascular shunt.

2. The smooth muscle sphincters regulate the blood flow to the capillary network by contracting to restrict blood flow to the network and relaxing to allow blood to flow in. The vascular shunt connects the arteriole and venule and allows blood to bypass the capillaries when the smooth muscle sphincters are contracted.

3 (a) Situation A would occur when the body is restricting blood flow to the capillaries, for example when trying to conserve heat by diverting blood away from the extremities.
   (b) Situation B would occur when the body is trying to remove excess heat by diverting blood to the skin and extremities or when the body is trying to provide extra blood to areas of high metabolism, e.g. when exercising or digesting food.

4. A portal venous system drains blood from one capillary network into another. An example is the hepatic portal system which drains blood from the capillary network in the gut lumen to the capillary network in the liver. Normally capillary networks drain into veins that return directly to the heart.

Formation of Tissue Fluid (page 230)

1. Tissue fluid bathes the tissues, providing oxygen and nutrients as well as a medium for the transport (away) of metabolic wastes, e.g. CO_2.

2. Capillary walls are thin enough (endothelium is only one cell thick) to allow substances to move easily in and out by diffusion.

3. (a) Arteriolar end: Hydrostatic pressure predominates in causing fluid to move out of the capillaries.
   (b) Venous end: Increased concentration of solutes and reduction in hydrostatic pressure at the venous end of a capillary bed **lowers the solute potential** within the capillary and there is a tendency for water and solutes to re-enter the capillary.

4. (a) Most tissue fluid finds it way directly back into the capillaries as a result of net inward pressure at the venule end of the capillary bed.
   (b) The lymph vessels (which parallel the blood system) drain tissue fluid (as lymph) back into the heart, thereby returning it into the main circulation.

Root Structure (page 231)

1. Any three of the following:
   - Roots anchor the plant into the soil
   - Absorb water and inorganic nutrients from the soil.
   - Sites for production of hormones gibberellins and cytokinins, which influence growth and development.
   - Specialised roots can have a variety of roles including supporting stems (prop roots), or supplying oxygen to underwater roots (pneumatophores) in the case of mangroves.

2. (a) and (b), any two of:
   - The primary xylem forms a star shape in the root centre (with usually 3 or 4 points).
   - The vascular tissue forms a central cylinder through the root (stele).
   - The stele is surrounded by a pericycle.

3. **Root hairs** increase the surface area for absorption.

4. The endodermis comprises a single layer of cells with a waterproof suberin coating along two sides. This waterproofing forces water to flow in one direction, into the vascular cylinder, rather than into the cortex.

Uptake at the Root (page 232)

1. (a) Passive absorption of minerals along with the water and active transport.
   (b) Apoplastic pathway (about 90%): Moving through the spaces within the cellulose cell wall. Symplastic pathway: Moving through the cell cytoplasm from cell to cell via plasmodesmata.

2. Large water uptake allows plants to take up sufficient quantities of minerals from the soil. These are often in very low concentration in the soil and low water uptakes would not provide adequate quantities.

3. (a) The **casparian strip** represents a waterproof barrier to water flow through the apoplastic pathway into the stele. It forces the water to move into the cells (i.e. move via the symplastic route).
   (b) This feature enables the plant to better regulate its uptake of ions, i.e. take up ions selectively. The movement of ions through the apoplast cannot be regulated because the flow does not occur across any partially permeable membranes.

Transpiration (page 233)

1. (a) They take up water by the roots.
   (b) – Transpiration stream enables plants to absorb sufficient quantities of the minerals they need (the minerals are absorbed with the water and are often in low concentration in the soil).
   – Transpiration helps cool the plant.

2. Water moves by osmosis in all cases. In any order:
   (a) **Transpiration pull**: Photosynthesis and evaporative loss of water from leaf surfaces create a more negative water potential in the leaf cells than elsewhere in the plant, facilitating movement of water along a gradient in water potential towards the site of evaporation (stomata).
   (b) **Capillary effect/cohesion-adhesion**: Water molecules cling together and adhere to the xylem, creating an unbroken water column through the plant. The upward pull on the sap creates a tension that facilitates movement of water up the plant.
   (c) **Root pressure** provides a weak push effect for upward water movement.

3. (a)-(c) any of the following: High wind, high light, high temperature, low humidity. All increase the rate of evaporation from the leaves.

4. The system excludes air. As the plant loses water through transpiration, it takes up water from the flask via roots (or cut stem). The volume removed from the flask by the plant is withdrawn from the pipette; this can be measured on the pipette graduations.

5. (a) Measurements were taken at the start and at the end of the experiment in the same conditions (still air, light shade, 20°C). These rates should be the same (give or take experimental error). This indicates that the plant has not been damaged by the experiment and any results are therefore a real response to the experimental conditions.
   (b) Moving air and bright sunlight increase transpiration rate, because they increase the rate of evaporation from the leaves. **Note**: Lower humidity could also be said to increase transpiration rate (by increasing the gradient in water potential), but this would need to be tested further, i.e. the results here do not conclusively show this. Another test where the effects of darkness and humidity level were separated would be required. This is a good discussion point for students investigating experimental design and interpretation of results.
   (c) Still, humid conditions reduce evaporative loss, dark conditions stop photosynthetic production of sugars (therefore solute concentration in the leaves falls). Both these reduce transpiration rate by reducing the concentration gradient for water movement.

KEY TERMS: Mix and Match (page 235)

Apoplastic pathway (O), Bulk flow (L), Capillary action (Y), Casparian strip (D), Cohesion-tension hypothesis (E), Carbon dioxide (N), Cellular respiration (P), Circulatory fluids (J), Countercrrent flow (I), Endodermis (T), Extraction rate (C), Gas exchange (Q), Gills (X), Guard cells (W), Osmosis (A), Oxygen (R), Respiratory gas (B), Root pressure (M), Stomata (Z), Symplastic pathway (U), Spiracles (F), Tracheae (G), Transpiration (S), Transpiration pull (H), Xylem (K)

The New Tree of Life (page 237)

1. The argument for the new classification as three domains is based on the fact that the genetic differences between the Bacteria and the Archaea are at least as great as between the Eukarya and the Bacteria. In other words, the traditional scheme does not accurately reflect the true evolutionary (genetic) relationship between the three groupings.

2. Any one of:
   – The eukaryote groups are given much less prominence, reflecting the true diversity of the prokaryote groups.
   – The Archaea have been separated out as distinct from other bacteria in order to reflect their uniqueness and indicate their true relationship to eukaryotes and to other prokaryotes.

3. The six kingdom classification scheme splits the prokaryotes into the kingdoms Eubacteria and Archaebacteria. These taxa are the same two domains that the three domain classification system uses.

The Species Concept (page 238)

1. Behavioural (they show no interest in each other).

2. Physical barrier; sea separating Australia from SE Asia.

3. The red wolf is rare and may have difficulty finding another member of its species to mate with.

4. The populations on the two land masses, which have identical appearance and habitat requirements, were connected relatively recently by a land bridge during the last ice age (about 18 000 years ago). This would have permitted breeding between the populations. Individuals from the current populations have been brought together and are able to interbreed and produce fertile offspring.

Protein Homologies (page 239)

1. Chimpanzees and gorillas have virtually identical amino acid sequences to humans for some proteins.

2. (a) They play a crucial role in the respiratory pathway. Most changes are likely to be deleterious so they change very little over time.
   (b) Such proteins are good candidates for use in establishing homologies because the few changes that are retained through time are likely to be meaningful, i.e. represent major divergences in evolutionary lines.

3. Any of: The rate of change must be calibrated against material evidence (e.g. fossils) for firm conclusions to be made. The functions of the protein may change over time. Clock may run at a different rate in different species.

DNA Homologies (page 241)

1. The similarity of DNA from different species can be established in a rudimentary way by measuring how closely single strands from each species mesh together. The more similar the DNA, the harder it is to separate them. These studies have confirmed most evolutionary relationships guessed at from anatomical comparisons.

2. Molecular evidence, especially based on highly conserved sequences, may be more accurate than classifications based solely on morphology because: (1) it is more objective than morphological determinations and (2) it is independent of coevolutionary influences. Plants with particular niche requirements often have similar morphological adaptations that are the result of coevolution and not shared ancestry, and these may cause them to be grouped together. The use of molecular evidence avoids the confusion potentially posed by adaptation and emphasises the most parsimonious (least complicated) phylogeny as is required by modern biological systematics.

Behaviour and Species Recognition (page 242)

1. (a) **Courtship** behaviour is a means of assessing the suitability, quality, and readiness of a mate and an effective way of ensuring reproductive isolation. it also has a role in reducing natural intraspecific aggression in the potential mate.
   (b) Stereotypical behaviors are easily recognised and will elicit appropriate (and equally recognisable) behaviours in the prospective mate.

2. Effective courtship provides a way to ensure that species do not mistakenly waste resources by mating with another species. This helps to ensure the production of viable offspring and maintains the integrity of the species gene pool.

Phylogenetic Systematics (page 243)

1. (a) Morphology recognises the importance of physical features in distinguishing between groups of organisms (it is a simpler and more familiar operation). It also recognises the amount of morphological change that occurs in species after their divergence from a common ancestor.
   (b) Biochemical evidence produces phylogenies that more correctly represent the true evolutionary relationships between groups (taxa).

2. A shared characteristic does not necessarily imply a related characteristic. For example spines on cacti and certain Euphorbia species. A shared derived characteristic is one that is shared between related species and their common ancestor, e.g. hair and its various forms in mammals (horns, quills etc).

3. Parsimony requires that the evolutionary history with the least number of evolutionary events be taken as the most likely (and most likely to be correct) history.

4. Biochemical evidence compares DNA and proteins between species and provides a more direct measure of common inheritance.

5. Data match 5. The mutation from C to T must have occurred separately in pig and whale/hippo ancestors.

6. (a) Pongidae   (b) Hominidae

Classification System (page 245)

1. (a) 1. Kingdom   (b) 1. Animal
       2. Phylum   2. Chordata
       3. Class   3. Mammalia
       4. Order   4. Primates
       5. Family   5. Hominidae
       6. Genus   6. *Homo*
       7. Species   7. *sapiens*

2. A two part naming system where the first word (capitalised and italicised) denotes the genus and the second word (lower case and italicised) denotes the species. Sometimes a third word (also lower case and italicised) denotes a subspecies.

3. (a) and (b) in any order:
   Avoid confusion over the use of common names for organisms; provide a unique name for each type of organism; attempt to determine/define the evolutionary relationship of organisms (phylogeny).

4. Any of the following:
   DNA profiling/sequencing: Where the unique genetic makeup of an individual is revealed and used for comparisons with related organisms.
   DNA hybridisation: Where the percentage DNA similarity between organisms is compared.
   Amino acid sequencing: Where the number of amino acid differences between organisms are compared.
   Immunological distance: Indirectly estimate the degree of similarity of proteins in different species.

5. (a) **Monotreme**: Egg laying with little internal development before laying, most development takes place in the egg
   (b) **Marsupial**: Birth takes place after limited internal development. Most development occurs after 'foetus' moves to the pouch and attaches to the nipple.
   (c) **Placental**: Long period of internal development, sustained by placenta. Birth takes place at highly developed stage.

KEY TERMS: Crossword (page 247)

Answers Across
1. Fungi
7. Cladogram
9. Distinguishing feature
12. Binomial nomenclature
14. Courtship
18. Synapomorphy
19. Homology
20. Prokaryotae
21. Class
22. Eubacteria

Answers Down
2. Genus
3. Plantae
4. Molecular clock
5. Protoctista
6. Order
8. Phylogeny
10. Morphology
11. Kingdom
13. Phylum
15. Family
16. Species
17. Archaea

Antibiotics and Resistance (page 249)

1. Ideally, an antimicrobial drug should have selective toxicity, targeting and killing the pathogen without harming the host. There is a wide range of antibiotics available; broad spectrum antibiotics, effective against a wide range of bacteria, are useful when the identity of the pathogen is unknown and a treatment decision must be made quickly. Narrow spectrum antibiotics

are useful when the pathogen is known and can be targeted directly. The latter are the preferred choice as they limit the disturbance to the body's own microbial flora. Some patients exhibit side effects, ranging from discomfort to anaphylaxis, but the vast majority of people experience few difficulties with their use.

2. (a) **Antibiotic resistance** refers to the resistance some bacteria develop to antibiotics that would normally inhibit their growth or kill them. In other words, they no longer show a reduction in growth response in the presence of the antibiotic.
   (b) It is important to finish a course of antibiotics so that the chances of survival of resistant mutants are minimised. If the course ends too quickly, more resistant cells may survive and flourish when antibiotic levels in the blood fall.

3. (a) **Bacteriostatic antibiotics** inhibit the growth of bacteria by interfering with protein production, DNA replication, or other aspects of their metabolism. They do not kill the bacteria. **Bacteriocidal antibiotics** kill the bacterial cells outright. The mode of action is often to inhibit the formation of the cell wall, to break the cell wall, or damage the plasma membrane.
   (b) **Bacteriostatic:** Chloramphenicol is a bacteriostatic antibiotic to *S. pneumoniae*. Bacterial numbers remain constant, there is no growth or reduction in numbers.
   Bacteriocidal: Ampicillin is bacteriocidal to *S. pneumoniae*. Bacterial numbers are rapidly reduced after exposure to this antibiotic.

4. (a) Antibiotic A is the most effective antibiotic because it produced the largest zone of clearance.
   (b) Disc 3 (5.5 µg ml^{-1}) and disc 4 (7 µg ml^{-1}) both had the same level of activity (they produced the same zone of clearance). However, Disc 3 is the most effective because it provides the same response as disc 4 but at a lower concentration.

Evolution of Drug Resistance (page 241)

1. Antibiotic resistance refers to the resistance bacteria show to antibiotics that would normally inhibit their growth. In other words, they no longer show a reduction in growth response in the presence of the antibiotic.

3. Widespread antibiotic resistance has implications for the treatment and control of what have been, in the past, quite easily treated diseases. Tuberculosis is one good example. Historically, it was effectively treated with antibiotics, but complacency over its control has lead to increasing multiple drug resistance in the *Mtb* population and a resurgence in the number of TB cases. This has huge implications for public health because more people live with (resistant forms of) the disease and spread it to more people as a result. In addition, the costs associated with treating TB are now also much higher.

In general, increasing resistance increases the costs lowers the efficacy of treating disease.

The Basis of Resistance (page 252)

1. Horizontal gene transmission describes the transfer of genetic material directly between bacteria by conjugation, transduction, or transformation. Vertical gene transmission describes the passing of genetic information from generation to generation by cell division.

2. When bacteria acquire several different mechanisms of resistance there is a much greater chance that they will become resistant to different classes of antibiotics. If this occurs, the treatment options against that particular pathogen are greatly reduced.

Global Biodiversity (page 253)

1. Species diversity refers to the number of different species within an area (species richness), while genetic diversity describes the diversity of genes within a particular species. Biodiversity is defined as the measure of all genes, species, and ecosystems in a region, so both genetic and species diversity are important in determining a region's total biodiversity.

2. Consideration of ecosystem diversity is very important when considering areas to set aside for conservation purposes because regions with diverse ecosystems will have higher levels of species richness, and the two measures are interdependent. A loss of habitat diversity will have a negative impact on the species richness of an area, and habitat diversity itself is contingent on species richness. Loss or decline in one will invariably result in loss or decline in the other.

3. The hotspot list is as follows:

1 **Tropical Andes**
The richest and most diverse hotspot where it is home to 20 000 endemic plants and at least 1500 endemic non-fish vertebrates.

2 **Sundaland**
Some of the largest islands in the world are found here in Southeast Asia. The second-richest hotspot in endemic plants, and well known for its mammalian fauna, which includes the orangutan.

3 **Mediterranean basin**
The site of many ancient and modern civilisations, it is the archetype and largest of the five Mediterranean-climate hotspots (also see nos. 9, 12, 19 and 22). One of the hotspots most heavily affected by human activity, it has 13 000 endemic plants, and is home to a number of interesting vertebrates such as the Spanish ibex.

4 **Madagascar and Indian Ocean islands**
Madagascar is a top conservation priority as this 'mini-continent' has undergone extensive deforestation. This hotspot is famous for reptiles such as chameleons and is home to all the world's lemur species.

5 **Indo-Burma**
An area stretching from the eastern slopes of the Himalayas through Burma and Thailand to Indochina. This region hosts the world's highest freshwater turtle diversity (43 species), and a diverse array of mammals. Several new ungulate species, such as the saola and giant muntjac, were recently discovered here.

6 **Caribbean**
One of the highest concentrations of species per unit area on Earth. Reptiles are particularly diverse (497 species are found here), 80 percent of which are found nowhere else. Non-fish vertebrates number 1518.

7 **Atlantic Forest region**
Once covering an area nearly three times the size of California, the Atlantic Forest has been reduced to about 7% of its original extent. It is most famous for 25 different kinds of primates, 20 of which are endemic. Among its best-known 'flagship species' are the critically endangered muriquis and lion tamarins.

8 **Philippines**
The most devastated of the hotspots, the forest cover has been reduced to 3% of its original extent. The Philippines is especially rich in endemic mammals and birds, such as the Philippine eagle.

9 **Cape Floristic Province**
This Mediterranean-type hotspot in southern Africa covers an area roughly the size of Ireland, and is now approximately 20% of its original extent. It is home to 8200 plant species, more than 5500 of which are endemic.

10 **Mesoamerica**
Forming a land bridge between two American continents, this hotspot features species representative of North and South America as well as its own unique biota. The spider and howler monkeys, Baird's tapir and unusual horned guan are 'flagship species'.

11 **Brazilian Cerrado**
A vast area of savanna and dry forest, the Cerrado is Brazil's new agricultural frontier and has been greatly altered by human activity in the past few decades. Home to 4400 endemic plants and several well-known mammal species, including the giant anteater, Brazilian tapir, and maned wolf.

12 **Southwest Australia**
A Mediterranean-type system, this hotspot is rich in endemic plants, reptiles, and marsupials including numbat, honey possum and quokka. It is also home to some of the world's tallest trees, e.g. giant eucalyptus.

13 **Mountains of South-Central China**
An area of extreme topography, these mountains are home to several of the world's best-known mammals, including the giant panda, the red panda, and the golden monkey. This hotspot is largely unexplored and may hold many undiscovered species.

14 **Polynesia/Micronesia**
This hotspot comprises thousands of tiny islands scattered over the vast Pacific, from Fiji and Hawaii to Easter Island and is noteworthy for its land snails, birds, and reptiles. Hawaii has suffered some of the most severe extinctions in modern history, due in part to the introduction of non-native plant and animal species.

15 **New Caledonia**
One of the smallest hotspots yet it has the largest concentration of unique plants with five plant families found nowhere else on Earth. This hotspot also features many endemic birds, such as the kagu, a long-legged, flightless forest dweller representing an entire family.

16 **Choco-Darien Western Ecuador**
Some of the world's wettest rain forests are found here, and amphibians, plants and birds are particularly abundant. It has one of the highest levels of endemism of any hotspot with 210 endemic amphibian species of the 350 species found here.

17 **Guinean Forests of West Africa**
(in error, this hotspot was not numbered on the map). With the highest mammalian diversity of any hotspot, these forests are home to the rare pygmy hippopotamus and many other striking species, including the western chimpanzee, Diana monkey and several forest duikers. The numbers of these endemic mammals have been severely reduced by large-scale logging and hunting.

18 **Western Ghats/Sri Lanka**
The Western Ghats mountain chain and adjacent island of Sri Lanka harbour high concentrations of endemic reptiles; of 259 reptile species, 161 are found nowhere else on Earth. This hotspot is also home to a number of 'flagship species', including the lion-tailed macaque.

19 **California Floristic Province**
Extending along the coast of California and into Oregon and northwestern Baja California, Mexico, this is one of five hotspots featuring a Mediterranean-type climate of hot, dry summers and cool, wet winters. It is especially rich in plants, with more than 4000 plant species, almost half of which are endemic.

20 **Succulent Karoo**
The only arid hotspot, the Succulent Karoo of southern Africa is renowned for unique succulent plants, as well as lizards and tortoises. in Namaqualand, in the southern part of this hotspot, a seasonal burst of bloom in September attracts many tourists.

21 **New Zealand**
This hotspot claims a number of world-famous endemic bird species, including kiwi (a nocturnal, flightless bird), takahe (a diurnal, flightless bird), and the critically endangered kakapo (a large, flightless parrot).

22 **Central Chile**
This hotspot features an arid region as well as a more typical Mediterranean-type zone. Best known for its incredible variety of plant species but also features unusual fauna, including one of the largest birds in the Americas, the Andean condor.

23 **Caucasus**
Situated between the Black Sea and the Caspian Sea, Caucasus habitats range from temperate forests to grasslands. A diversity of plants have been recorded here with some 6300 species, more than 1600 of which are endemic.

24 **Wallacea**
Named for the 19th century naturalist Alfred Russel Wallace, this hotspot comprises the large Indonesian island of Sulawesi, the Moluccas and many smaller islands. The area is particularly rich in endemic mammals and birds.

25 **Eastern Arc Mountains/ Coastal Forests of Tanzania and Kenya**
A chain of upland and coastal forests, this hotspot claims one of the densest concentrations of endemic plant and primate species in the world. It is home to African violets and 4000 other plant species, as well as the 1500 remaining Kirk's red colobus monkeys.

Loss of Biodiversity (page 254)

1. Loss of biodiversity from an ecosystem has a cascade effect to the remaining species. The effects depend very much on the species that disappears (e.g. predator, producer) but, in general, species loss results in altered food chains and food webs, allowing for the proliferation of some species and the demise of others. Other changes include a loss of stability and resilience, and disruption to normal processes, interactions and outcomes, such as nutrient cycling, soil formation, pollination, oxygen production, carbon sequestration and climate regulation.

Britain's Biodiversity (page 255)

1. Table and graph below:

	% of species		Key
Protozoa	22.8%	(82°)	
Algae	22.8%	(82°)	
Fungi	17.1%	(62°)	
Ferns & bryophytes	1.2%	(4°)	
Lichens	1.7%	(6°)	
Flowering plants	1.6%	(6°)	
Invertebrates	32.5%	(117°)	
Vertebrates	0.3%	(1°)	

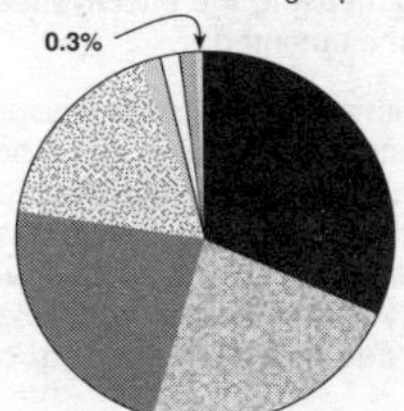

Proportion of British species in different taxonomic groups

2. Invertebrate phyla, protozoans, algae, and lower plants show a much higher biodiversity (as measured by number of identified species) than the higher plants and vertebrate taxa.

3. (a) Our knowledge of the biodiversity (as measured by number of identified species) of invertebrate animals and bacteria (especially the latter) is poor compared with that of vertebrates i.e. there are many more undescribed species, and there is considerable doubt as to how many species actually exist.

   (b) Vertebrates are large, conspicuous organisms with (for the most part) sexual reproduction. This makes determination of "a species" relatively simple even if morphology is similar. **Note**: Many invertebrates and bacteria are as yet undescribed and there is much doubt as to what constitutes a species in those organisms that rarely reproduce sexually. This is especially the case for bacteria, where species classification tends to based upon criteria other than the ability to interbreed. For invertebrates that normally reproduce by parthenogenesis, identification of type specimens (specimens representing the species) is particularly difficult. Morphology may be very similar between different species and species distinction may be based only on physiological or genetic criteria.

4. The UK has a low level of endemism. It is not far from the European continent ; this facilitates species transfers. In addition, its isolation from the continental land mass has been limited for much of its geologic history (isolation is required for endemism to develop).

5. (a) 12 000 − 3800 = 8200
   8200 ÷ 12 000 X 100 = 68.3%. Nearly 70% decline.

   (b) The barn owl is widely distributed, so the population does not have the problems associated with scattered or isolated distribution. The causes of decline have been identifiable and manageable in that rather simple measures can be taken to increase survival rates of both the young and breeding adults. They are also relatively adaptable birds, taking a variety of prey and responding well to habitat enhancement (e.g. using new nest sites).

Measuring Diversity (page 257)

1. (a) **Species richness** measures the number of species within an ecosystem, whereas **species evenness** describes how equally the species are distributed within an ecosystem.

   (b) Both measures are important when considering species conservation. Species richness could give an indication of ecosystem stability, and therefore how at-risk particular species may be. Species evenness provides an indication of the species distribution (a limited distribution or a distribution where individuals are widely separated may indicate the species is at risk).

2. Sampling must be carried out in an unbiased manner which provides a true representation of the ecosystem. This is usually achieved by random sampling techniques. The sample size must be large enough to gather a true representation of the species present, and the sampling method used must be suitable for capturing information of the species likely to be present.

3. High diversity systems have a greater number of biotic interactions operating to buffer them against change (the loss or decline of one component (species) is less likely to affect the entire ecosystem). With a large number of species involved, ecosystem processes, such as nutrient recycling, are more efficient and less inclined to disruption.

4. **Keystone species** are pivotal to some important ecosystem function such as production of biomass or nutrient recycling. Because their role is disproportionately large, their removal has a similarly disproportionate effect on ecosystem function.

5. Species diversity index used in (any of):
   - Comparisons of similar ecosystems which have been subjected to (beneficial or detrimental) human influence (e.g. restoration or pollution).
   - Assessment of the same ecosystem before and after some event (fire, flood, pollution, environmental restoration).
   - Assessment of the same ecosystem along some environmental gradient (e.g. distance from a point

source of pollution).
- Assessment of the biodiversity value of an area for the purposes of management or preservation (tends to be a political lobbying point).

6. (a) DI = 37 x 36 ÷ ((7 x 6) + (10 x 9) + (11 x 10) + (2 x 1) + (4 x 3) + (3 x 2)) = 1332 ÷ 262 = 5.08
   (b) Without any frame of reference (e.g. for a known high or low diversity system), no reasonable comment can be made about the diversity of this ecosystem. Herein lies the problem with an index that has no theoretical upper boundary.

Tropical Deforestation (page 259)

1. (a) They enhance removal of carbon dioxide from the atmosphere (anti-greenhouse).
   (b) They maintain species diversity.
   (c) They have, as-yet-undiscovered, potentially useful species for medicines etc.

2. Tropical deforestation has three primary causes: Logging, fires, and road-building (associated with clearance for agriculture). Logging and fires destroy forest. Intrusion of roads into pristine forested areas allows the invasion of weed species, increases erosion, and prevents the reestablishment of forest species. Agriculture maintains cleared areas and prevents forest reestablishment. Lengthy continued agriculture on thin tropical soils precludes the easy reestablishment of forest once the agricultural land has been abandoned.

Hedgerows: An Ancient Tradition (page 260)

1. (a)-(c) any advantages of:
   - Hedgerows provide habitat and food for wildlife.
   - Hedgerows act as corridors along which animals can move between regions of suitable habitat (e.g. for feeding). Corridors are also important for the establishment and expansion of some plant species.
   - Hedgerows shelter stock and reduce wind speed, thereby reducing erosion.
   - Hedgerows provide habitat for the predators of prey species and pollinating insects. This may benefit the farmer.

2. Hedgerows might be regarded by a farmer as undesirable because:
   - Hedgerows hamper effective use of some farm machinery.
   - Hedgerows take up space that could otherwise be used for grazing or crop production.
   - Hedgerows provide habitat for competitors to grazing livestock (e.g. hares) and predators (foxes).

3. Retaining well managed hedgerows offers the farmer many benefits. Hedges provide shelter for stock and reduce wind speeds, which stops erosion. Hedges provide habitat for helpful bird and insect species, which can prey on harmful pest insects and prevent spikes in pest populations. The also prevent the spread of wind-borne insect pests. Well managed hedges are also and eco-friendly cost-effective alternative to other types of fencing.

Agriculture and Diversity (page 261)

1. (a) Advantage 1: High yields are maintained by intensive farming even though some areas are retired from production.
   (b) Advantage 2: There is a financial incentive if certain areas are left as conservation estate (income from tourism related to conservation areas and direct compensation for loss of income from land turned over to conservation).
   (c) Disadvantage: Intensive farming practices may have a lasting detrimental impact on surrounding conservation estate. The financial rewards of conserving land may not compensate for the income lost through having unproductive land.

2. (a) Habitat loss (hedgerows and woodland areas).
   (b) Decline in abundance and diversity of food sources associated with habitat loss.

3. (a)
   - Hedgerow legislation to preserve existing hedgerow habitats.
   - Policies to preserve or restore woodland cover in previously wooded areas (afforestation).
   - Schemes (with financial incentives) to encourage environmentally sensitive farming practices.
   (b) Environmental impact assessments and biodiversity estimates would determine the biodiversity levels and the environmental damage in certain habitats (e.g. areas with hedgerows vs areas where they had been removed or had become unkempt). This would identify areas requiring implementation of the biodiversity policies mentioned above, and also provide a baseline to measure the effectiveness of the strategies once implemented.

4. Retaining areas of uncultivated meadow alongside intensively managed pasture is helpful in that it boosts biodiversity in the area and can benefit agriculture in providing habitat for helpful insects, such as predators of pest species and pollinators such as bumblebees. High diversity systems cycle nutrients more efficiently, reducing fertiliser costs, and have better soil structure.